The Diary of Anne Frank

and Related Readings

McDougal Littell
A HOUGHTON MIFFLIN COMPANY

Evanston, Illinois   Boston   Dallas

Acknowledgments

Random House, Inc.: *The Diary of Anne Frank, A Play* by Frances Goodrich and Albert Hackett. Copyright © 1956 by Frances Goodrich and Albert Hackett. Copyright renewed 1984 by Albert Hackett. Reprinted by arrangement with Random House, Inc. Caution: *The Diary of Anne Frank* is the sole property of the estate of the dramatists and is fully protected by copyright. It may not be acted by professionals or amateurs without written permission and the payment of a royalty. All rights, including professional, amateur, stock, radio broadcasting, television, motion picture, recitation, lecturing, public reading, and the rights of translation into foreign languages are reserved. All inquiries should be addressed to the agent for the estate of the dramatists: Leah Salisbury, 234 West 44th Street, New York, NY.

Doubleday: Excerpts from *Anne Frank: Diary of a Young Girl* by Anne Frank. Copyright 1952 by Otto H. Frank. Reprinted by permission of Doubleday, a division of Bantam Doubleday Dell Publishing Group, Inc.

Simon & Schuster, Inc.: Excerpt from *Anne Frank Remembered* by Miep Gies with Alison Leslie Gold. Copyright © 1987 by Miep Gies and Alison Leslie Gold. Reprinted by permission of Simon & Schuster, Inc.

Continued on page 200.

Cover photo: © by ANNE FRANK-Fonds, Basel, Switzerland.
Author photo: AP/Wide World Photos.

Printed in the U.S.A.

2002 Impression.
Copyright © 1997 by McDougal Littell Inc. All rights reserved.

ISBN-13: 978-0-395-83364-3
ISBN-10: 0-395-83364-7

31   1083   14

4500461181

Contents

The Diary of Anne Frank

Dramatized by
Frances Goodrich
and **Albert Hackett**

Based upon the book
ANNE FRANK: DIARY OF A YOUNG GIRL

Characters

Mr. Frank

Miep

Mrs. Van Daan

Mr. Van Daan

Peter Van Daan

Mrs. Frank

Margot Frank

Anne Frank

Mr. Kraler

Mr. Dussel

The Time:
During the years of World War II
and immediately thereafter.

The Place: Amsterdam

Act One

....

Scene I

The scene remains the same throughout the play. It is the top floor of a warehouse and office building in Amsterdam, Holland. The sharply peaked roof of the building is outlined against a sea of other rooftops, stretching away into the distance. Nearby is the belfry of a church tower, the Westertoren, whose carillon rings out the hours. Occasionally faint sounds float up from below: the voices of children playing in the street, the tramp of marching feet, a boat whistle from the canal.

The three rooms of the top floor and a small attic space above are exposed to our view. The largest of the rooms is in the center, with two small rooms, slightly raised, on either side. On the right is a bathroom, out of sight. A narrow steep flight of stairs at the back leads up to the attic. The rooms are sparsely furnished with a few chairs, cots, a table or two. The windows are painted over, or covered with makeshift blackout curtains. In the main room there is a sink, a gas ring for cooking and a wood-burning stove for warmth.

The room on the left is hardly more than a closet. There is a skylight in the sloping ceiling. Directly under this room is a small steep stairwell, with steps leading down to a door. This is the only entrance from the building below. When the door is opened we see that it has been concealed on the outer side by a bookcase attached to it.

(The curtain rises on an empty stage. It is late afternoon November, 1945.

The rooms are dusty, the curtains in rags. Chairs and tables are overturned.

The door at the foot of the small stairwell swings open. Mr. Frank comes up the steps into view. He is a gentle, cultured European in his middle years. There is still a trace of a German accent in his speech.

He stands looking slowly around, making a supreme effort at self-control. He is weak, ill. His clothes are threadbare.

After a second he drops his rucksack on the couch and moves slowly about. He opens the door to one of the smaller rooms, and then abruptly closes it again, turning away. He goes to the window at the back, looking off at the Westertoren as its carillon strikes the hour of six, then he moves restlessly on.

From the street below we hear the sound of a barrel organ and children's voices at play. There is a many-colored scarf hanging from a nail. Mr. Frank takes it, putting it around his neck. As he starts back for his rucksack, his eye is caught by something lying on the floor. It is a woman's white glove. He holds it in his hand and suddenly all of his self-control is gone. He breaks down, crying.

We hear footsteps on the stairs. Miep Gies comes up, looking for Mr. Frank. Miep is a Dutch girl of about twenty-two. She wears a coat and hat, ready to go home. She is pregnant. Her attitude toward Mr. Frank is protective, compassionate.)

Miep. Are you all right, Mr. Frank?

Mr. Frank (*Quickly controlling himself*). Yes, Miep, yes.

Miep. Everyone in the office has gone home . . . It's after six. (*Then pleading*) Don't stay up here, Mr. Frank. What's the use of torturing yourself like this?

Mr. Frank. I've come to say good-bye . . . I'm leaving here, Miep.

Miep. What do you mean? Where are you going? Where?

Mr. Frank. I don't know yet. I haven't decided.

Miep. Mr. Frank, you can't leave here! This is your home! Amsterdam is your home. Your business is here, waiting for you . . . You're needed here . . . Now that the war is over, there are things that . . .

Mr. Frank. I can't stay in Amsterdam, Miep. It has too many memories for me. Everywhere there's something . . . the house we lived in . . . the school . . . that street organ playing out there . . . I'm not the person you used to know, Miep. I'm a bitter old man. (*Breaking off*) Forgive me. I shouldn't speak to you like this . . . after all that you did for us . . . the suffering . . .

Miep. No. No. It wasn't suffering. You can't say we suffered. (*As she speaks, she straightens a chair which is overturned.*)

Mr. Frank. I know what you went through, you and Mr. Kraler. I'll remember it as long as I live. (*He gives one last look around.*) Come, Miep.

(*He starts for the steps, then remembers his rucksack, going back to get it.*)

Miep (*Hurrying up to a cupboard*). Mr. Frank, did you see? There are some of your papers here. (*She brings a bundle of papers to him.*) We found them in a heap of rubbish on the floor after . . . after you left.

Mr. Frank. Burn them.

(*He opens his rucksack to put the glove in it.*)

Miep. But, Mr. Frank, there are letters, notes . . .

Mr. Frank. Burn them. All of them.

Miep. Burn this?

(*She hands him a paperbound notebook.*)

Mr. Frank (*Quietly*). Anne's diary. (*He opens the diary and begins to read.*) "Monday, the sixth of July, nineteen forty-two." (*To* Miep) Nineteen forty-two. Is it possible, Miep? . . . Only three years ago. (*As he continues his reading, he sits down on the couch.*) "Dear Diary, since you and I are going to be great friends, I will start by telling you about myself. My name is Anne Frank. I am thirteen years old. I was born in Germany the twelfth of June, nineteen twenty-nine. As my family is Jewish, we emigrated to Holland when Hitler came to power."

(*As* Mr. Frank *reads on, another voice joins his, as if coming from the air. It is* Anne's *voice.*)

Mr. Frank *and* **Anne.** "My father started a business, importing spice and herbs. Things went well for us until nineteen forty. Then the war came, and the Dutch capitulation, followed by the arrival of the Germans. Then things got very bad for the Jews."

(*Mr. Frank's voice dies out. Anne's voice continues alone. The lights dim slowly to darkness. The curtain falls on the scene.*)

Anne's Voice. You could not do this and you could not

do that. They forced Father out of his business. We had to wear yellow stars. I had to turn in my bike. I couldn't go to a Dutch school any more. I couldn't go to the movies, or ride in an automobile, or even on a streetcar, and a million other things. But somehow we children still managed to have fun. Yesterday Father told me we were going into hiding. Where, he wouldn't say. At five o'clock this morning Mother woke me and told me to hurry and get dressed. I was to put on as many clothes as I could. It would look too suspicious if we walked along carrying suitcases. It wasn't until we were on our way that I learned where we were going. Our hiding place was to be upstairs in the building where Father used to have his business. Three other people were coming in with us . . . the Van Daans and their son Peter . . . Father knew the Van Daans but we had never met them . . .

(During the last lines the curtain rises on the scene. The lights dim on. Anne's voice fades out.)

Scene II

It is early morning, July, 1942. The rooms are bare, as before, but they are now clean and orderly.

Mr. Van Daan, a tall, portly man in his late forties, is in the main room, pacing up and down, nervously smoking a cigarette. His clothes and overcoat are expensive and well cut.

Mrs. Van Daan sits on the couch, clutching her possessions, a hatbox, bags, etc. She is a pretty woman in her early forties. She wears a fur coat over her other clothes.

Peter Van Daan is standing at the window of the room on the right, looking down at the street below. He is a shy, awkward boy of sixteen. He wears a cap, a raincoat, and long Dutch trousers, like "plus fours." At his feet is a black case, a carrier for his cat.

The yellow Star of David is conspicuous on all of their clothes.

Mrs. Van Daan (*Rising, nervous, excited*). Something's happened to them! I know it!

Mr. Van Daan. Now, Kerli!

Mrs. Van Daan. Mr. Frank said they'd be here at seven o'clock. He said . . .

Mr. Van Daan. They have two miles to walk. You can't expect . . .

Mrs. Van Daan. They've been picked up. That's what's happened. They've been taken . . .

(Mr. Van Daan *indicates that he hears someone coming.*)

Mr. Van Daan. You see?

(Peter *takes up his carrier and his schoolbag, etc., and goes into the main room as* Mr. Frank *comes up the stairwell from below.* Mr. Frank *looks much younger now. His movements are brisk, his manner confident. He wears an overcoat and carries his hat and a small cardboard box. He crosses to the Van Daans, shaking hands with each of them.*)

Mr. Frank. Mrs. Van Daan, Mr. Van Daan, Peter. (*Then, in explanation of their lateness*) There were too many of the Green Police on the streets . . . we had to take the long way around.

(*Up the steps come* Margot Frank, Mrs. Frank, Miep (*not pregnant now*) *and* Mr. Kraler. *All of them carry bags, packages, and so forth. The Star of David is conspicuous on all of the* Franks' *clothing.* Margot *is eighteen, beautiful, quiet, shy.* Mrs. Frank *is a young mother, gently bred, reserved. She, like* Mr. Frank, *has a slight German accent.* Mr. Kraler *is a Dutchman, dependable, kindly.*

As Mr. Kraler *and* Miep *go upstage to put down their parcels,* Mrs. Frank *turns back to call* Anne.)

Mrs. Frank. Anne?

(Anne *comes running up the stairs. She is thirteen, quick in her movements, interested in everything, mercurial in her emotions. She wears a cape, long wool socks and carries a schoolbag.*)

Mr. Frank (*Introducing them*). My wife, Edith. Mr. and Mrs. Van Daan (Mrs. Frank *hurries over, shaking hands with them.*) . . . their son, Peter . . . my daughters, Margot and Anne.

(Anne *gives a polite little curtsy as she shakes* Mr. Van Daan's *hand. Then she immediately starts off on a tour of investigation of her new home, going upstairs to the attic room.*

Miep *and Mr. Kraler* *are putting the various things they have brought on the shelves.*)

Mr. Kraler. I'm sorry there is still so much confusion.

Mr. Frank. Please. Don't think of it. After all, we'll have plenty of leisure to arrange everything ourselves.

Miep (*To* Mrs. Frank). We put the stores of food you sent in here. Your drugs are here . . . soap, linen here.

Mrs. Frank. Thank you, Miep.

Miep. I made up the beds . . . the way Mr. Frank and Mr. Kraler said. (*She starts out.*) Forgive me. I have to hurry. I've got to go to the other side of town to get some ration books for you.

Mrs. Van Daan. Ration books? If they see our names on ration books, they'll know we're here.

Mr. Kraler. There isn't anything . . .

Miep. Don't worry. Your names won't be on them. (*As she hurries out*) I'll be up later.

Mr. Frank. Thank you, Miep.

Mrs. Frank (*To* Mr. Kraler). It's illegal, then, the ration books? We've never done anything illegal.

Mr. Frank. We won't be living here exactly according to regulations. (*As* Mr. Kraler *reassures* Mrs. Frank, *he takes various small things, such as matches, soap, etc., from his pockets, handing them to her.*)

Mr. Kraler. This isn't the black market, Mrs. Frank. This is what we call the white market . . . helping all of the hundreds and hundreds who are hiding out in Amsterdam.

(*The carillon is heard playing the quarter-hour before eight.*

Mr. Kraler *looks at his watch.* Anne *stops at the window as she comes down the stairs.*)

Anne. It's the Westertoren!

Mr. Kraler. I must go. I must be out of here and downstairs in the office before the workmen get here. (*He starts for the stairs leading out.*) Miep or I, or both of us, will be up each day to bring you food and news and find out what your needs are. Tomorrow I'll get you a better bolt for the door at the foot of the stairs. It needs a bolt that you can throw yourself and open only at our signal. (*To Mr. Frank*) Oh . . . You'll tell them about the noise?

Mr. Frank. I'll tell them.

Mr. Kraler. Good-bye then for the moment. I'll come up again, after the workmen leave.

Mr. Frank. Good-bye, Mr. Kraler.

Mrs. Frank (*Shaking his hand*). How can we thank you? (*The others murmur their good-byes.*)

Mr. Kraler. I never thought I'd live to see the day when a man like Mr. Frank would have to go into hiding. When you think— (*He breaks off, going out. Mr. Frank follows him down the steps, bolting the door after him. In the interval before he returns,* Peter *goes over to* Margot, *shaking hands with her. As* Mr. Frank *comes back up the steps,* Mrs. Frank *questions him anxiously.*)

Mrs. Frank. What did he mean, about the noise?

Mr. Frank. First let us take off some of these clothes. (*They all start to take off garment after garment. On each of their coats, sweaters, blouses, suits, dresses, is another yellow Star of David. Mr. and Mrs. Frank are underdressed* *quite simply. The others wear several things, sweaters, extra dresses, bathrobes, aprons, nightgowns, etc.)*

Mr. Van Daan. It's a wonder we weren't arrested, walking along the streets . . . Petronella with a fur coat in July . . . and that cat of Peter's crying all the way.

Anne *(As she is removing a pair of panties)*. A cat?

Mrs. Frank *(Shocked)*. Anne, please!

Anne. It's all right. I've got on three more. *(She pulls off two more. Finally, as they have all removed their surplus clothes, they look to* Mr. Frank, *waiting for him to speak.)*

Mr. Frank. Now. About the noise. While the men are in the building below, we must have complete quiet. Every sound can be heard down there, not only in the workrooms, but in the offices too. The men come at about eight-thirty, and leave at about five-thirty. So, to be perfectly safe, from eight in the morning until six in the evening we must move only when it is necessary, and then in stockinged feet. We must not speak above a whisper. We must not run any water. We cannot use the sink, or even, forgive me, the w.c. The pipes go down through the workrooms. It would be heard. No trash . . . *(Mr. Frank stops abruptly as he hears the sound of marching feet from the street below. Everyone is motionless, paralyzed with fear.* Mr. Frank *goes quietly into the room on the right to look down out of the window.* Anne *runs after him, peering out with him. The tramping feet pass without stopping. The tension is relieved.* Mr. Frank, *followed by* Anne, *returns to the main room and resumes his intructions to the group)* . . . No trash must ever be thrown out which might reveal that someone is living up here . . . not even a potato paring. We must burn everything in the stove at night. This is the way we must live until it is over, if we are to survive.

(*There is silence for a second.*)

Mrs. Frank. Until it is over.

Mr. Frank. (*Reassuringly*). After six we can move about . . . we can talk and laugh and have our supper and read and play games . . . just as we would at home. (*He looks at his watch.*) And now I think it would be wise if we all went to our rooms, and were settled before eight o'clock. Mrs. Van Daan, you and your husband will be upstairs. I regret that there's no place up there for Peter. But he will be here, near us. This will be our common room, where we'll meet to talk and eat and read, like one family.

Mr. Van Daan. And where do you and Mrs. Frank sleep?

Mr. Frank. This room is also our bedroom.

Mrs. Van Daan. That isn't right. We'll sleep here and you take the room upstairs.

Mr. Van Daan. It's your place.

Mr. Frank. Please. I've thought this out for weeks. It's the best arrangement. The only arrangement.

Mrs. Van Daan (*To* Mr. Frank). Never, never can we thank you. (*Then to* Mrs. Frank) I don't know what would have happened to us, if it hadn't been for Mr. Frank.

Mr. Frank. You don't know how your husband helped me when I came to this country . . . knowing no one . . . not able to speak the language. I can never repay him for that. (*Going to* Van Daan) May I help you with your things?

Mr. Van Daan. No. No. (*To* Mrs. Van Daan) Come along, liefje.

Mrs. Van Daan. You'll be all right, Peter? You're not afraid?

Peter (*Embarrassed*). Please, Mother.

(*They start up the stairs to the attic room above.* Mr. Frank *turns to* Mrs. Frank.)

Mr. Frank. You too must have some rest, Edith. You didn't close your eyes last night. Nor you, Margot.

Anne. I slept, Father. Wasn't that funny? I knew it was the last night in my own bed, and yet I slept soundly.

Mr. Frank. I'm glad, Anne. Now you'll be able to help me straighten things in here. (*To* Mrs. Frank *and* Margot) Come with me . . . You and Margot rest in this room for the time being. (*He picks up their clothes, starting for the room on the right.*)

Mrs. Frank. You're sure . . . ? I could help . . . And Anne hasn't had her milk . . .

Mr. Frank. I'll give it to her. (*To* Anne *and* Peter) Anne, Peter . . . it's best that you take off your shoes now, before you forget. (*He leads the way to the room, followed by* Margot.)

Mrs. Frank. You're sure you're not tired, Anne?

Anne. I feel fine. I'm going to help Father.

Mrs. Frank. Peter, I'm glad you are to be with us.

Peter. Yes, Mrs. Frank.

(Mrs. Frank *goes to join* Mr. Frank *and* Margot.)

(*During the following scene* Mr. Frank *helps* Margot *and* Mrs. Frank *to hang up their clothes. Then he persuades them both to lie down and rest. The* Van Daans *in their room above settle themselves. In the main room* Anne *and* Peter *remove their shoes.* Peter *takes his cat out of the carrier.*)

Anne. What's your cat's name?

Peter. Mouschi.

Anne. Mouschi! Mouschi! Mouschi! (*She picks up the cat, walking away with it. To* Peter) I love cats. I have one . . . a darling little cat. But they made me leave her behind. I left some food and a note for the neighbors to take care of her . . . I'm going to miss her terribly. What is yours? A him or a her?

Peter. He's a tom. He doesn't like strangers. (*He takes the cat from her, putting it back in its carrier.*)

Anne (*Unabashed*). Then I'll have to stop being a stranger, won't I? Is he fixed?

Peter (*Startled*). Huh?

Anne. Did you have him fixed?

Peter. No.

Anne. Oh, you ought to have him fixed—to keep him from—you know, fighting. Where did you go to school?

Peter. Jewish Secondary.

Anne. But that's where Margot and I go! I never saw you around.

Peter. I used to see you . . . sometimes . . .

Anne. You did?

Peter. . . . in the school yard. You were always in the middle of a bunch of kids. (*He takes a penknife from his pocket.*)

Anne. Why didn't you ever come over?

Peter. I'm sort of a lone wolf. (*He starts to rip off his Star of David.*)

Anne. What are you doing?

Peter. Taking it off.

Anne. But you can't do that. They'll arrest you if you go out without your star.

(*He tosses his knife on the table.*)

Peter. Who's going out?

Anne. Why, of course! You're right! Of course we don't need them any more. (*She picks up his knife and starts to take her star off.*) I wonder what our friends will think when we don't show up today?

Peter. I didn't have any dates with anyone.

Anne. Oh, I did. I had a date with Jopie to go and play ping-pong at her house. Do you know Jopie de Waal?

Peter. No.

Anne. Jopie's my best friend. I wonder what she'll think when she telephones and there's no answer? . . . Probably she'll go over to the house . . . I wonder what she'll think . . . we left everything as if we'd suddenly been called away . . . breakfast dishes in the sink . . . beds not made . . . (*As she pulls off her star, the cloth underneath shows clearly the color and form of the star.*) Look! It's still there! (Peter *goes over to the stove with his star.*) What're you going to do with yours?

Peter. Burn it.

Anne (*She starts to throw hers in, and cannot.*). It's funny, I can't throw mine away. I don't know why.

Peter. You can't throw . . . ? Something they branded you with . . . ? That they made you swear so they could spit on you?

Anne. I know. I know. But after all, it is the Star of David, isn't it?

(*In the bedroom, right,* Margot *and* Mrs. Frank *are lying down.* Mr. Frank *starts quietly out.*)

Peter. Maybe it's different for a girl.

(Mr. Frank *comes into the main room.*)

Mr. Frank. Forgive me, Peter. Now let me see. We must find a bed for your cat. (*He goes to a cupboard.*) I'm glad you brought your cat. Anne was feeling so badly about hers. (*Getting a used small washtub*) Here we are. Will it be comfortable in that?

Peter (*Gathering up his things*). Thanks.

Mr. Frank (*Opening the door of the room on the left*). And here is your room. But I warn you, Peter, you can't grow any more. Not an inch, or you'll have to sleep with your feet out of the skylight. Are you hungry?

Peter. No.

Mr. Frank. We have some bread and butter.

Peter. No, thank you.

Mr. Frank. You can have it for luncheon then. And tonight we will have a real supper . . . our first supper together.

Peter. Thanks. Thanks.

(*He goes into his room. During the following scene he arranges his possessions in his new room.*)

Mr. Frank. That's a nice boy, Peter.

Anne. He's awfully shy, isn't he?

Mr. Frank. You'll like him, I know.

Anne. I certainly hope so, since he's the only boy I'm likely to see for months and months.

(Mr. Frank *sits down, taking off his shoes.*)

Mr. Frank. Annele, there's a box there. Will you open it? (*He indicates a carton on the couch.* Anne *brings it to the center table. In the street below there is the sound of children playing.*)

Anne (*As she opens the carton*). You know the way I'm going to think of it here? I'm going to think of it as a boarding house. A very peculiar summer boarding house, like the one that we— (*She breaks off as she pulls out some photographs.*) Father! My movie stars! I was wondering where they were! I was looking for them this morning . . . and Queen Wilhelmina! How wonderful!

Mr. Frank. There's something more. Go on. Look further. (*He goes over to the sink, pouring a glass of milk from a thermos bottle.*)

Anne (*Pulling out a pasteboard-bound book*). A diary! (*She throws her arms around her father.*) I've never had a diary. And I've always longed for one. (*She looks around the room.*) Pencil, pencil, pencil, pencil. (*She starts down the stairs.*) I'm going down to the office to get a pencil.

Mr. Frank. Anne! No! (*He goes after her, catching her by the arm and pulling her back.*)

Anne (*Startled*). But there's no one in the building now.

Mr. Frank. It doesn't matter. I don't want you ever to go beyond that door.

Anne (*Sobered*). Never . . . ? Not even at nighttime, when everyone is gone? Or on Sundays? Can't I go down to listen to the radio?

Mr. Frank. Never. I am sorry, Anneke. It isn't safe. No, you must never go beyond that door.

(*For the first time* Anne *realizes what "going into hiding" means.*)

Anne. I see.

Mr. Frank. It'll be hard, I know. But always remember this, Anneke. There are no walls, there are no bolts, no locks that anyone can put on your mind. Miep will bring us books. We will read history, poetry, mythology. (*He gives her the glass of milk.*) Here's your milk. (*With his arm about her, they go over to the couch, sitting down side by side.*) As a matter of fact, between us, Anne, being here has certain advantages for you. For instance, you remember the battle you had with your mother the other day on the subject of overshoes? But in the end you had to wear them? Well now, you see, for as long as we are here you will never have to wear overshoes! Isn't that good? And the coat that you inherited from Margot, you won't have to wear that any more. And the piano! You won't have to practice on the piano. I tell you, this is going to be a fine life for you!

(Anne's *panic is gone.* Peter *appears in the doorway of his room, with a saucer in his hand. He is carrying his cat.*)

Peter. I . . . I . . . I thought I'd better get some water for Mouschi before . . .

Mr. Frank. Of course.

(*As he starts toward the sink the carillon begins to chime the hour of eight. He tiptoes to the window at the back and looks down at the street below. He turns to* Peter, *indicating in pantomime that it is too late.* Peter *starts back for his room. He steps on a creaking board. The three of them are frozen for a minute in fear. As* Peter *starts away again,* Anne *tiptoes over to him and pours some of the milk from her glass into the saucer for the cat.* Peter *squats on the floor, putting the milk before the cat.* Mr. Frank *gives* Anne *his fountain pen, and then goes into the room at the right. For a second* Anne *watches the cat, then she goes over to the center table, and opens her diary.*

In the room at the right, Mrs. Frank *has sat up quickly at the sound of the carillon.* Mr. Frank *comes in and sits down beside her on the settee, his arm comfortingly around her.*

Upstairs, in the attic room, Mr. *and* Mrs. Van Daan *have hung their clothes in the closet and are now seated on the iron bed.* Mrs. Van Daan *leans back exhausted.* Mr. Van Daan *fans her with a newspaper.*

Anne *starts to write in her diary. The lights dim out, the curtain falls.*

In the darkness Anne's *voice comes to us again, faintly at first, and then with growing strength.*)

Anne's Voice. I expect I should be describing what it feels like to go into hiding. But I really don't know yet myself. I only know it's funny never to be able to go outdoors . . . never to breathe fresh air . . . never to run and shout and jump. It's the silence in the nights that frightens me most. Every time I hear a creak in the house, or a step on the street outside, I'm sure they're coming for us. The days aren't so bad. At least we know that Miep and Mr. Kraler are down there below us in the office. Our protectors, we call them. I asked Father what would happen to them if the Nazis found out they were hiding us. Pim said that they would suffer the same fate that we would . . . Imagine! They know this, and yet when they come up here, they're always cheerful and gay as if there were nothing in the world to bother them . . . Friday, the twenty-first of August, nineteen forty-two. Today I'm going to tell you our general news. Mother is unbearable. She insists on treating me like a baby, which I loathe. Otherwise things are going better. The weather is . . .

(As Anne's voice is fading out, the curtain rises on the scene.)

Anns brother

It is a little after six o'clock in the evening, two months later.

Margot *is in the bedroom at the right, studying. Mr. Van Daan is lying down in the attic room above.*

The rest of the "family" is in the main room. Anne *and* Peter *sit opposite each other at the center table, where they have been doing their lessons.* Mrs. Frank *is on the couch.* Mrs. Van Daan *is seated with her fur coat, on which she has been sewing, in her lap. None of them are wearing their shoes.*

Their eyes are on Mr. Frank, *waiting for him to give them the signal which will release them from their day-long quiet.* Mr. Frank, *his shoes in his hand, stands looking down out of the window at the back, watching to be sure that all of the workmen have left the building below.*

After a few seconds of motionless silence, Mr. Frank *turns from the window.*

Mr. Frank (*Quietly, to the group*). It's safe now. The last workman has left. (*There is an immediate stir of relief.*)

Anne (*Her pent-up energy explodes*). WHEE! *excited*

Mrs. Frank (*Startled, amused*). Anne!

Mrs. Van Daan. I'm first for the w.c. (*She hurries off to the bathroom.* Mrs. Frank *puts on her shoes and starts up to the sink to prepare supper.* Anne *sneaks* Peter's *shoes from under the table and hides them behind her back.* Mr. Frank *goes in to* Margot's *room.*)

Mr. Frank (*To* Margot). Six o'clock. School's over.

(Margot *gets up, stretching.* Mr. Frank *sits down to put on his shoes. In the main room* Peter *tries to find his.*)

Peter (*To* Anne). Have you seen my shoes?

Anne (*Innocently*). Your shoes?

Peter. You've taken them, haven't you?

Anne. I don't know what you're talking about.

Peter. You're going to be sorry!

Anne. Am I? (Peter *goes after her.* Anne, *with his shoes in her hand, runs from him, dodging behind her mother.*)

Mrs. Frank (*Protesting*). Anne, dear!

Peter. Wait till I get you!

Anne. I'm waiting! (Peter *makes a lunge for her. They both fall to the floor.* Peter *pins her down, wrestling with her to get the shoes.*) Don't! Don't! Peter, stop it. Ouch!

Mrs. Frank. Anne! . . . Peter!

(*Suddenly* Peter *becomes self-conscious. He grabs his shoes roughly and starts for his room.*)

Anne (*Following him*). Peter, where are you going? Come dance with me.

Peter. I tell you I don't know how.

Anne. I'll teach you. ⟶ *very excited*

Peter. I'm going to give Mouschi his dinner.

Anne. Can I watch?

Peter. He doesn't like people around while he eats.

Anne. Peter, please.

Peter. No! (*He goes into his room.* Anne *slams his door after him.*)

Mrs. Frank. Anne, dear, I think you shouldn't play like that with Peter. It's not dignified.

Anne. Who cares if it's dignified? I don't want to be dignified.

(Mr. Frank *and* Margot *come from the room on the right.* Margot *goes to help her mother.* Mr. Frank *starts for the center table to correct* Margot's *school papers.*)

Upset

Mrs. Frank (*To* Anne). You complain that I don't treat you like a grownup. But when I do, you resent it.

Anne. I only want some fun . . . someone to laugh and clown with . . . After you've sat still all day and hardly moved, you've got to have some fun. I don't know what's the matter with that boy.

Mr. Frank. He isn't used to girls. Give him a little time.

Anne. Time? Isn't two months time? I could cry. (*Catching hold of* Margot) Come on, Margot . . . dance with me. Come on, please.

Margot. I have to help with supper.

Anne. You know we're going to forget how to dance . . . When we get out we won't remember a thing.

Veryclose

(*She starts to sing and dance by herself.* Mr. Frank *takes her in his arms, waltzing with her.* Mrs. Van Daan *comes in from the bathroom.*)

Mrs. Van Daan. Next? (*She looks around as she starts putting on her shoes.*) Where's Peter?

Anne (*As they are dancing*). Where would he be!

Mrs. Van Daan. He hasn't finished his lessons, has he? His father'll kill him if he catches him in there with that cat and his work not done. (Mr. Frank *and* Anne *finish their dance. They bow to each other with extravagant formality.*) Anne, get him out of there, will you?

Anne (*At* Peter's *door*). Peter? Peter?

Peter (*Opening the door a crack*). What is it?

Anne. Your mother says to come out.

Peter. I'm giving Mouschi his dinner.

Mrs. Van Daan. You know what your father says. (*She sits on the couch, sewing on the lining of her fur coat.*)

Peter. For heaven's sake, I haven't even looked at him since lunch.

Mrs. Van Daan. I'm just telling you, that's all.

Anne. I'll feed him.

Peter. I don't want you in there.

Mrs. Van Daan. Peter!

Peter (*To* Anne). Then give him his dinner and come right out, you hear? (*He comes back to the table.* Anne *shuts the door of* Peter's *room after her and disappears behind the curtain covering his closet.*)

Mrs. Van Daan (*To* Peter). Now is that any way to talk to your little girl friend?

Peter. Mother . . . for heaven's sake . . . will you please stop saying that?

Mrs. Van Daan. Look at him blush! Look at him!

Peter. Please! I'm not . . . anyway . . . let me alone, will you?

Mrs. Van Daan. He acts like it was something to be ashamed of. It's nothing to be ashamed of, to have a little girl friend.

Peter. You're crazy. She's only thirteen.

Mrs. Van Daan. So what? And you're sixteen. Just perfect. Your father's ten years older than I am. (*To Mr. Frank*) I warn you, Mr. Frank, if this war lasts much longer, we're going to be related and then . . .

Mr. Frank. Mazeltov! *Anne and Peter are going to be married*

Mrs. Frank (*Deliberately changing the conversation*). I wonder where Miep is. She's usually so prompt.

(*Suddenly everything else is forgotten as they hear the sound of an automobile coming to a screeching stop in the street below. They are tense, motionless in their terror. The car starts away. A wave of relief sweeps over them. They pick up their occupations again. Anne flings open the door of Peter's room, making a dramatic entrance. She is dressed in Peter's clothes. Peter looks at her in fury. The others are amused.*)

All have sense of fear

Anne. Good evening, everyone. Forgive me if I don't stay. (*She jumps up on a chair.*) I have a friend waiting for me in there. My friend Tom. Tom Cat. Some people say that we look alike. But Tom has the most beautiful whiskers, and I have only a little fuzz. I am hoping . . . in time . . .

Peter. All right, Mrs. Quack Quack!

Anne (*Outraged—jumping down*) Peter!

Peter. I heard about you . . . How you talked so much in class they called you Mrs. Quack Quack. How Mr. Smitter made you write a composition . . . "'Quack, quack,' said Mrs. Quack Quack."

Anne. Well, go on. Tell them the rest. How it was so good he read it out loud to the class and then read it to all his other classes!

Peter. Quack! Quack! Quack . . . Quack . . . Quack . . .

(*Anne pulls off the coat and trousers.*)

Anne. You are the most intolerable, insufferable boy I've ever met!

(*She throws the clothes down the stairwell. Peter goes down after them.*)

Peter. Quack, quack, quack!

Mrs. Van Daan (*To* Anne). That's right, Anneke! Give it to him!

Anne. With all the boys in the world . . . Why I had to get locked up with one like you! . . .

Peter. Quack, quack, quack, and from now on stay out of my room!

(*As* Peter *passes her,* Anne *puts out her foot, tripping him. He picks himself up, and goes on into his room.*)

Mrs. Frank (*Quietly*). Anne, dear . . . your hair. (*She feels* Anne's *forehead.*) You're warm. Are you feeling all right?

Anne. Please, Mother. (*She goes over to the center table, slipping into her shoes.*)

Mrs. Frank (*Following her*). You haven't a fever, have you?

Anne (*Pulling away*). No. No.

Mrs. Frank. You know we can't call a doctor here, ever. There's only one thing to do . . . watch carefully. Prevent an illness before it comes. Let me see your tongue.

Anne. Mother, this is perfectly absurd.

Mrs. Frank. Anne, dear, don't be such a baby. Let me see your tongue. (*As* Anne *refuses,* Mrs. Frank *appeals to* Mr. Frank.) Otto . . . ?

Mr. Frank. You hear your mother, Anne. (*Anne flicks out her tongue for a second, then turns away.*)

Mrs. Frank. Come on—open up! (*As Anne opens her mouth very wide*) You seem all right . . . but perhaps an aspirin . . .

Mrs. Van Daan. For heaven's sake, don't give that child any pills. I waited for fifteen minutes this morning for her to come out of the w.c.

Anne. I was washing my hair!

Mr. Frank. I think there's nothing the matter with our Anne that a ride on her bike, or a visit with her friend Jopie deWaal wouldn't cure. Isn't that so, Anne?

He protects her

(*Mr. Van Daan comes down into the room. From outside we hear faint sounds of bombers going over and a burst of ack-ack.*)

Mr. Van Daan. Miep not come yet?

Mrs. Van Daan. The workmen just left, a little while ago.

Mr. Van Daan. What's for dinner tonight?

Mrs. Van Daan. Beans.

—Limited

Mr. Van Daan. Not again!

Mrs. Van Daan. Poor Putti! I know. But what can we do? That's all that Miep brought us.

(*Mr. Van Daan starts to pace, his hands behind his back. Anne follows behind him, imitating him.*)

Anne. We are now in what is known as the "bean cycle." Beans boiled, beans en casserole, beans with strings, beans without strings . . .

(Peter *has come out of his room. He slides into his place at the table, becoming immediately absorbed in his studies.*)

Mr. Van Daan (*To* Peter). I saw you . . . in there, playing with your cat.

Mrs. Van Daan. He just went in for a second, putting his coat away. He's been out here all the time, doing his lessons.

Mr. Frank (*Looking up from the papers*). Anne, you got an excellent in your history paper today . . . and very good in Latin.

Anne (*Sitting beside him*). How about algebra?

Mr. Frank. I'll have to make a confession. Up until now I've managed to stay ahead of you in algebra. Today you caught up with me. We'll leave it to Margot to correct.

Anne. Isn't algebra *vile*, Pim!

Mr. Frank. Vile!

Margot (*To* Mr. Frank). How did I do?

Anne (*Getting up*). Excellent, excellent, excellent, excellent!

Mr. Frank (To Margot). You should have used the subjunctive here . . .

Margot. Should I? . . . I thought . . . look here . . . I didn't use it here . . . (*The two become absorbed in the papers.*)

Anne. Mrs. Van Daan, may I try on your coat?

Mrs. Frank. No, Anne.

Mrs. Van Daan (*Giving it to* Anne). It's all right . . . but careful with it. (Anne *puts it on and struts with it.*)

My father gave me that the year before he died. He always bought the best that money could buy.

Anne. Mrs. Van Daan, did you have a lot of boy friends before you were married? *wants advice*

Mrs. Frank. Anne, that's a personal question. It's not *curious* courteous to ask personal questions.

Mrs. Van Daan. Oh I don't mind. (*To* Anne) Our house was always swarming with boys. When I was a girl we had . . .

Mr. Van Daan. Oh, God. Not again!

Mrs. Van Daan (*Good-humored*). Shut up! (*Without a pause, to* Anne. Mr. Van Daan *mimics* Mrs. Van Daan, *speaking the first few words in unison with her.*) One summer we had a big house in Hilversum. The boys came buzzing round like bees around a jam pot. And when I was sixteen! . . . We were wearing our skirts very short those days and I had good-looking legs. (*She pulls up her skirt, going to* Mr. Frank.) I still have 'em. I may not be as pretty as I used to be, but I still have my legs. How about it, Mr. Frank?

Mr. Van Daan. All right. All right. We see them.

Mrs. Van Daan. I'm not asking you. I'm asking Mr. Frank.

Peter. Mother, for heaven's sake.

Mrs. Van Daan. Oh, I embarrass you, do I? Well, I just hope the girl you marry has as good. (*Then to* Anne) My father used to worry about me, with so many boys hanging round. He told me, if any if them gets fresh, you say to him . . . "Remember, Mr. So-and-So, remember I'm a lady."

Anne. "Remember, Mr. So-and-So, remember I'm a lady." (*She gives* Mrs. Van Daan *her coat.*)

Mr. Van Daan. Look at you, talking that way in front of her! Don't you know she puts it all down in that diary?

Mrs. Van Daan. So, if she does? I'm only telling the truth!

(Anne *stretches out, putting her ear to the floor, listening to what is going on below. The sound of the bombers fades away.*)

Mrs. Frank (*Setting the table*). Would you mind, Peter, if I moved you over to the couch?

Anne (*Listening*). Miep must have the radio on.

(Peter *picks up his papers, going over to the couch beside* Mrs. Van Daan.)

Mr. Van Daan (*Accusingly, to* Peter). Haven't you finished yet?

Peter. No.

Mr. Van Daan. You ought to be ashamed of yourself.

Peter. All right. All right. I'm a dunce. I'm a hopeless case. Why do I go on?

Mrs. Van Daan. You're not hopeless. Don't talk that way. It's just that you haven't anyone to help you, like the girls have. (*To* Mr. Frank) Maybe you could help him, Mr. Frank?

Mr. Frank. I'm sure that his father . . . ?

Mr. Van Daan. Not me. I can't do anything with him. He won't listen to me. You go ahead . . . if you want.

Mr. Frank (*Going to* Peter). What about it, Peter? Shall we make our school coeducational?

Mrs. Van Daan (*Kissing* Mr. Frank). You're an angel, Mr. Frank. An angel. I don't know why I didn't meet you before I met that one there. Here, sit down, Mr. Frank . . . (*She forces him down on the couch beside* Peter.) Now, Peter, you listen to Mr. Frank.

Mr. Frank. It might be better for us to go into Peter's room. (Peter *jumps up eagerly, leading the way.*)

Mrs. Van Daan. That's right. You go in there, Peter. You listen to Mr. Frank. Mr. Frank is a highly educated man. (*As* Mr. Frank *is about to follow* Peter *into his room,* Mrs. Frank *stops him and wipes the lipstick from his lips. Then she closes the door after them.*)

Anne (*On the floor, listening*). Shh! I can hear a man's voice talking.

Mr. Van Daan (*To* Anne). Isn't it bad enough here without your sprawling all over the place? (Anne *sits up.*)

Mrs. Van Daan (*To* Mr. Van Daan). If you didn't smoke so much, you wouldn't be so bad-tempered.

Mr. Van Daan. Am I smoking? Do you see me smoking?

Mrs. Van Daan. Don't tell me you've used up all those cigarettes.

Mr. Van Daan. One package. Miep only brought me one package.

Mrs. Van Daan. It's a filthy habit anyway. It's a good time to break yourself.

Mr. Van Daan. Oh, stop it, please.

Mrs. Van Daan. Will you shut up? (*During this,* Mrs. Frank *and* Margot *have studiously kept their eyes down. But* Anne, *seated on the floor, has been following the discussion interestedly.* Mr. Van Daan *turns to see her staring up at him.*) And what are you staring at?

Anne. I never heard grownups quarrel before. I thought only children quarreled.

Mr. Van Daan. This isn't a quarrel! It's a discussion. And I never heard children so rude before.

Anne (*Rising, indignantly*). I, rude!

He thinks Anne is annoying

Mr. Van Daan. Yes!

Mrs. Frank (*Quickly*). Anne, will you get me my knitting? (Anne *goes to get it.*) I must remember, when Miep comes, to ask her to bring me some more wool.

Margot (*Going to her room*). I need some hairpins and some soap. I made a list. (*She goes into her bedroom to get the list.*)

Mrs. Frank (*To* Anne). Have you some library books for Miep when she comes?

Anne. It's a wonder that Miep has a life of her own, the way we make her run errands for us. Please, Miep, get me some starch. Please take my hair out and have it cut. Tell me all the latest news, Miep. (*She goes over, kneeling on the couch beside* Mrs. Van Daan.) Did you know she was engaged? His name is Dirk, and Miep's afraid the Nazis will ship him off to Germany to work in one of their war plants. That's what they're doing with some of the young Dutchmen . . . they pick them up off the streets—

Mr. Van Daan (*Interrupting*). Don't you ever get tired of talking? Suppose you try keeping still for five minutes. Just five minutes. (*He starts to pace again. Again* Anne *follows him, mimicking him.* Mrs. Frank *jumps up and takes her by the arm up to the sink, and gives her a glass of milk.*)

Mrs. Frank. Come here, Anne. It's time for your glass of milk.

Mr. Van Daan. Talk, talk, talk. I never heard such a child. Where is my . . . ? Every evening it's the same, talk, talk, talk. (*He looks around.*) Where is my . . . ?

Mrs. Van Daan. What're you looking for?

Mr. Van Daan. My pipe. Have you seen my pipe?

Mrs. Van Daan. What good's a pipe? You haven't got any tobacco.

Mr. Van Daan. At least I'll have something to hold in my mouth! (*Opening* Margot's *bedroom door*) Margot, have you seen my pipe?

Margot. It was on the table last night. (Anne *puts her glass of milk on the table and picks up his pipe, hiding it behind her back.*)

Mr. Van Daan. I know. I know. Anne, did you see my pipe? . . . Anne!

Mrs. Frank. Anne, Mr. Van Daan is speaking to you.

Anne. Am I allowed to talk now?

Mr. Van Daan. You're the most aggravating . . . The trouble with you is, you've been spoiled. What you need is a good old-fashioned spanking.

Anne (*Mimicking* Mrs. Van Daan). "Remember, Mr. So-and-So, remember I'm a lady." (*She thrusts the pipe into his mouth, then picks up her glass of milk.*)

Mr. Van Daan (*Restraining himself with difficulty*). Why aren't you nice and quiet like your sister Margot? Why do you have to show off all the time? Let me give you a little advice, young lady. Men don't like that kind of thing in a girl. You know that? A man likes a girl who'll listen to him once in a while . . . a domestic girl, who'll keep her house shining for her husband . . . who loves to cook and sew and . . .

Anne. I'd cut my throat first! I'd open my veins! I'm going to be remarkable! I'm going to Paris . . .

Mr. Van Daan (*Scoffingly*). Paris!

Anne. . . . to study music and art.

Mr. Van Daan. Yeah! Yeah!

Anne. I'm going to be a famous dancer or singer . . . or something wonderful. (*She makes a wide gesture, spilling the glass of milk on the fur coat in* Mrs. Van Daan's *lap*. Margot *rushes quickly over with a towel*. Anne *tries to brush the milk off with her skirt.*)

Mrs. Van Daan. Now look what you've done . . . you clumsy little fool! My beautiful fur coat my father gave me . . .

Anne. I'm so sorry.

Mrs. Van Daan. What do you care? It isn't yours . . . So go on, ruin it! Do you know what that coat cost? Do you? And now look at it! Look at it!

Anne. I'm very, very sorry.

Mrs. Van Daan. I could kill you for this. I could just kill you! (Mrs. Van Daan *goes up the stairs, clutching the coat*. Mr. Van Daan *starts after her.*)

Mr. Van Daan. Petronella . . . *liefje! Liefje!* . . . Come back . . . the supper . . . come back!

Mrs. Frank. Anne, you must not behave in that way.

Anne. It was an accident. Anyone can have an accident.

Mrs. Frank. I don't mean that. I mean the answering back. You must not answer back. They are our guests. We must always show the greatest courtesy to them. We're all living under terrible tension. (*She stops as* Margot *indicates that* Van Daan *can hear. When he is gone, she continues.*) That's why we must control ourselves . . . You don't hear Margot getting into arguments with them, do you? Watch Margot. She's always courteous with them. Never familiar. She keeps her distance. And they respect her for it. Try to be like Margot.

Anne. And have them walk all over me, the way they do her? No, thanks!

Mrs. Frank. I'm not afraid that anyone is going to walk all over you, Anne. I'm afraid for other people, that you'll walk on them. I don't know what happens to you, Anne. You are wild, self-willed. If I had ever talked to my mother as you talk to me . . . *What the parents want respect*

Anne. Things have changed. People aren't like that any more. "Yes, Mother." "No, Mother." "Anything you say, Mother." I've got to fight things out for myself! Make something of myself!

Mrs. Frank. It isn't necessary to fight to do it. Margot doesn't fight, and isn't she . . . ?

Anne (*Violently rebellious*). Margot! Margot! Margot! That's all I hear from everyone . . . how wonderful

Margot is . . . "Why aren't you like Margot?"

Margot (*Protesting*). Oh, come on, Anne, don't be so . . .

Anne (*Paying no attention*). Everything she does is right, and everything I do is wrong! I'm the goat around here! . . . You're all against me! . . . And you worst of all!

(*She rushes off into her room and throws herself down on the settee, stifling her sobs. Mrs. Frank sighs and starts toward the stove.*)

Mrs. Frank (*To* Margot). Let's put the soup on the stove . . . if there's anyone who cares to eat. Margot, will you take the bread out? (*Margot gets the bread from the cupboard.*) I don't know how we can go on living this way . . . I can't say a word to Anne . . . she flies at me . . .

Margot. You know Anne. In half an hour she'll be out here, laughing and joking. *They don't take her seriously*

Mrs. Frank. And . . . (*She makes a motion upwards, indicating the* Van Daans.) . . . I told your father it wouldn't work . . . but no . . . no . . . he had to ask them, he said . . . he owed it to him, he said. Well, he knows now that I was right! These quarrels! . . . This bickering!

Margot (*With a warning look*). Shush. Shush.

(*The buzzer for the door sounds. Mrs. Frank gasps, startled.*)

Mrs. Frank. Every time I hear that sound, my heart stops!

Margot (*Starting for* Peter's door). It's Miep. (*She knocks at the door.*) Father?

(Mr. Frank *comes quickly from* Peter's *room.*)

Mr. Frank. Thank you, Margot. (*As he goes down the steps to open the outer door*) Has everyone his list?

Margot. I'll get my books. (*Giving her mother a list.*) Here's your list. (Margot *goes into her and* Anne's *bedroom on the right.* Anne *sits up, hiding her tears, as* Margot *comes in.*) Miep's here.

(Margot *picks up her books and goes back.* Anne *hurries over to the mirror, smoothing her hair.*)

Mr. Van Daan (*Coming down the stairs*). Is it Miep?

Margot. Yes. Father's gone down to let her in.

Mr. Van Daan. At last I'll have some cigarettes!

Mrs. Frank (*To* Mr. Van Daan). I can't tell you how unhappy I am about Mrs. Van Daan's coat. Anne should never have touched it.

Mr. Van Daan. She'll be all right.

Mrs. Frank. Is there anything I can do?

Mr. Van Daan. Don't worry.

(*He turns to meet* Miep. *But it is not* Miep *who comes up the steps. It is* Mr. Kraler, *followed by* Mr. Frank. *Their faces are grave.* Anne *comes from the bedroom.* Peter *comes from his room.*)

Mrs. Frank. Mr. Kraler!

Mr. Van Daan. How are you, Mr. Kraler?

Margot. This is a surprise.

Mrs. Frank. When Mr. Kraler comes, the sun begins to shine.

Mr. Van Daan. Miep is coming?

Mr. Kraler. Not tonight.

(Kraler *goes to* Margot *and* Mrs. Frank *and* Anne, *shaking hands with them.*)

Mrs. Frank. Wouldn't you like a cup of coffee? . . . Or, better still, will you have supper with us?

Mr. Frank. Mr. Kraler has something to talk over with us. Something has happened, he says, which demands an immediate decision.

Mrs. Frank (*Fearful*). What is it?

(Mr. Kraler *sits down on the couch. As he talks he takes bread, cabbages, milk, etc., from his briefcase, giving them to* Margot *and* Anne *to put away.*)

Mr. Kraler. Usually, when I come up here, I try to bring you some bit of good news. What's the use of telling you the bad news when there's nothing that you can do about it? But today something has happened . . . Dirk . . . Miep's Dirk, you know, came to me just now. He tells me that he has a Jewish friend living near him. A dentist. He says he's in trouble. He begged me, could I do anything for this man? Could I find him a hiding place? . . . So I've come to you . . . I know it's a terrible thing to ask of you, living as you are, but would you take him in with you?

Mr. Frank. Of course we will.

Mr. Kraler (*Rising*). It'll be just for a night or two . . . until I find some other place. This happened so suddenly that I didn't know where to turn.

Mr. Frank. Where is he?

Mr. Kraler. Downstairs in the office.

Mr. Frank. Good. Bring him up.

Mr. Kraler. His name is Dussel . . . Jan Dussel.

Mr. Frank. Dussel . . . I think I know him.

Mr. Kraler. I'll get him. (*He goes quickly down the steps and out.* Mr. Frank *suddenly becomes conscious of the others.*)

Mr. Frank. Forgive me. I spoke without consulting you. But I knew you'd feel as I do.

Mr. Van Daan. There's no reason for you to consult anyone. This is your place. You have a right to do exactly as you please. The only thing I feel . . . there's so little food as it is . . . and to take in another person . . .

(Peter *turns away, ashamed of his father.*)

Mr. Frank. We can stretch the food a little. It's only for a few days.

Mr. Van Daan. You want to make a bet?

Mrs. Frank. I think it's fine to have him. But, Otto, where are you going to put him? Where?

Peter. He can have my bed. I can sleep on the floor. I wouldn't mind.

Mr. Frank. That's good of you, Peter. But your room's too small . . . even for *you*.

Anne. I have a much better idea. I'll come in here with you and Mother, and Margot can take Peter's room and Peter can go in our room with Mr. Dussel.

Margot. That's right. We could do that.

Mr. Frank. No, Margot. You mustn't sleep in that room . . . neither you nor Anne. Mouschi has caught some rats in there. Peter's brave. He doesn't mind.

Anne. Then how about *this*? I'll come in here with you and Mother, and Mr. Dussel can have my bed.

Mrs. Frank. No. No. *No!* Margot will come in here with us and he can have her bed. It's the only way. Margot, bring your things in here. Help her, Anne.

(Margot hurries into her room to get her things.)

Anne *(To her mother).* Why Margot? Why can't I come in here?

Mrs. Frank. Because it wouldn't be proper for Margot to sleep with a . . . Please, Anne. Don't argue. Please. *(Anne starts slowly away.)*

Mr. Frank *(To Anne).* You don't mind sharing your room with Mr. Dussel, do you, Anne?

Anne. No. No, of course not.

Mr. Frank. Good. *(Anne goes off into her bedroom, helping Margot. Mr. Frank starts to search in the cupboards.)* Where's the cognac?

Mrs. Frank. It's there. But, Otto, I was saving it in case of illness.

Mr. Frank. I think we couldn't find a better time to use it. Peter, will you get five glasses for me?

(Peter goes for the glasses. Margot comes out of her bedroom, carrying her possessions, which she hangs behind a curtain in the main room. Mr. Frank finds the cognac and pours it into the five glasses that Peter brings him. Mr. Van Daan stands looking on sourly. Mrs. Van Daan comes downstairs and looks around at all the bustle.)

Mrs. Van Daan. What's happening? What's going on?

Mr. Van Daan. Someone's moving in with us.

Mrs. Van Daan. In here? You're joking.

[handwritten in left margin: Anne is going to be with Jan]

Margot. It's only for a night or two . . . until Mr. Kraler finds him another place.

Mr. Van Daan. Yeah! Yeah!

(Mr. Frank *hurries over as* Mr. Kraler *and* Dussel *come up.* Dussel *is a man in his late fifties, meticulous, finicky . . . bewildered now. He wears a raincoat. He carries a briefcase, stuffed full, and a small medicine case.*)

Mr. Frank. Come in, Mr. Dussel.

Mr. Kraler. This is Mr. Frank.

Dussel. Mr. Otto Frank?

Mr. Frank. Yes. Let me take your things. (*He takes the hat and briefcase, but* Dussel *clings to his medicine case.*) This is my wife Edith . . . Mr. and Mrs. Van Daan . . . their son, Peter . . . and my daughters, Margot and Anne.

(Dussel *shakes hands with everyone.*)

Mr. Kraler. Thank you, Mr. Frank. Thank you all. Mr. Dussel, I leave you in good hands. Oh . . . Dirk's coat.

(Dussel *hurriedly takes off the raincoat, giving it to* Mr. Kraler. *Underneath is his white dentist's jacket, with a yellow Star of David on it.*)

Dussel (*To* Mr. Kraler). What can I say to thank you . . . ?

Mrs. Frank (*To* Dussel). Mr. Kraler and Miep . . . They're our life line. Without them we couldn't live.

Mr. Kraler. Please. Please. You make us seem very heroic. It isn't that at all. We simply don't like the Nazis. (*To* Mr. Frank, *who offers him a drink*) No, thanks. (*Then going on*) We don't like their methods. We don't like . . .

Mr. Frank (*Smiling*). I know. I know. "No one's going to tell us Dutchmen what to do with our damn Jews!"

Mr. Kraler (*To* Dussel). Pay no attention to Mr. Frank. I'll be up tomorrow to see that they're treating you right. (*To* Mr. Frank) Don't trouble to come down again. Peter will bolt the door after me, won't you, Peter?

Peter. Yes, sir.

Mr. Frank. Thank you, Peter. I'll do it.

Mr. Kraler. Good night. Good night.

Group. Good night, Mr. Kraler.

We'll see you tomorrow, etc., etc.

(Mr. Kraler *goes out with* Mr. Frank. Mrs. Frank *gives each one of the "grownups" a glass of cognac.*)

Mrs. Frank. Please, Mr. Dussel, sit down.

(Mr. Dussel *sinks into a chair.* Mrs. Frank *gives him a glass of cognac.*)

Dussel. I'm dreaming. I know it. I can't believe my eyes. Mr. Otto Frank here! (*To* Mrs. Frank) You're not in Switzerland then? A woman told me . . . She said she'd gone to your house . . . the door was open, everything was in disorder, dishes in the sink. She said she found a piece of paper in the wastebasket with an address scribbled on it . . . an address in Zurich. She said you must have escaped to Zurich.

Anne. Father put that there purposely . . . just so people would think that very thing!

Dussel. And you've been *here* all the time?

Mrs. Frank. All the time . . . ever since July.

(Anne *speaks to her father as he comes back.*)

Anne. It worked, Pim . . . the address you left! Mr. Dussel says that people believe we escaped to Switzerland.

Mr. Frank. I'm glad . . . And now let's have a little drink to welcome Mr. Dussel. (*Before they can drink, Mr. Dussel bolts his drink. Mr. Frank smiles and raises his glass.*) To Mr. Dussel. Welcome. We're very honored to have you with us.

Mrs. Frank. To Mr. Dussel, welcome.

(*The* Van Daans *murmur a welcome. The "grownups" drink.*)

Mrs. Van Daan. Um. That was good.

Mr. Van Daan. Did Mr. Kraler warn you that you won't get much to eat here? You can imagine . . . three ration books among the seven of us . . . and now you make eight.

(Peter *walks away, humiliated. Outside a street organ is heard dimly.*)

Dussel (*Rising*). Mr. Van Daan, you don't realize what is happening outside that you should warn me of a thing like that. You don't realize what's going on . . . (*As Mr. Van Daan starts his characteristic pacing, Dussel turns to speak to the others.*) Right here in Amsterdam every day hundreds of Jews disappear . . . They surround a block and search house by house. Children come home from school to find their parents gone. Hundreds are being deported . . . people that you and I know . . . the Hallensteins . . . the Wessels . . .

Mrs. Frank (*In tears*). Oh, no. No!

Dussel. They get their call-up notice . . . come to the Jewish theatre on such and such a day and hour . . . bring only what you can carry in a rucksack. And if you refuse the call-up notice, then they come and drag you from your home and ship you off to Mauthausen. The death camp!

Mrs. Frank. We didn't know that things had got so much worse.

Dussel. Forgive me for speaking so.

Anne (*Coming to* Dussel). Do you know the deWaals? . . . What's become of them? Their daughter Jopie and I are in the same class. Jopie's my best friend.

Dussel. They are gone. *— they have been captured*

Anne. Gone?

Dussel. With all the others.

Anne. Oh, no. Not Jopie!

(*She turns away, in tears.* Mrs. Frank *motions to* Margot *to comfort her.* Margot *goes to* Anne, *putting her arms comfortingly around her.*)

Mrs. Van Daan. There were some people called Wagner. They lived near us . . . ?

Mr. Frank (*Interrupting, with a glance at* Anne). I think we should put this off until later. We all have many questions we want to ask . . . But I'm sure that Mr. Dussel would like to get settled before supper.

Dussel. Thank you. I would. I brought very little with me.

Mr. Frank (*Giving him his hat and briefcase*). I'm sorry we can't give you a room alone. But I hope you won't be too uncomfortable. We've had to make strict rules here . . . a schedule of hours . . . We'll tell you after supper. Anne, would you like to take Mr. Dussel to his room?

Anne (*Controlling her tears*). If you'll come with me, Mr. Dussel? (*She starts for her room.*)

Dussel (*Shaking hands with each in turn*). Forgive me if I haven't really expressed my gratitude to all of you. This has been such a shock to me. I'd always thought of myself as Dutch. I was born in Holland. My father was born in Holland, and my grandfather. And now . . . after all these years . . . (*He breaks off*) If you'll excuse me.

(Dussel *gives a little bow and hurries off after* Anne. Mr. Frank *and the others are subdued.*)

Anne (*Turning on the light*). Well, here we are.

(Dussel *looks around the room. In the main room* Margot *speaks to her mother.*)

Margot. The news sounds pretty bad, doesn't it? It's so different from what Mr. Kraler tells us. Mr. Kraler says things are improving.

Mr. Van Daan. I like it better the way Kraler tells it.

(*They resume their occupations, quietly.* Peter *goes off into his room. In* Anne's *room,* Anne *turns to* Dussel.)

Anne. You're going to share the room with me.

Dussel. I'm a man who's always lived alone. I haven't had to adjust myself to others. I hope you'll bear with me until I learn.

Anne. Let me help you. (*She takes his briefcase.*) Do you always live all alone? Have you no family at all?

Dussel. No one. (*He opens his medicine case and spreads his bottles on the dressing table.*)

Anne. How dreadful. You must be terribly lonely.

Dussel. I'm used to it.

Anne I don't think I could ever get used to it. Didn't you even have a pet? A cat, or a dog?

Dussel. I have an allergy for fur-bearing animals. They give me asthma.

Anne. Oh, dear. Peter has a cat.

Dussel. Here? He has it here?

Anne. Yes. But we hardly ever see it. He keeps it in his room all the time. I'm sure it will be all right.

Dussel. Let us hope so.

(*He takes some pills to fortify himself.*)

Anne. That's Margot's bed, where you're going to sleep. I sleep on the sofa there. (*Indicating the clothes hooks on the wall*) We cleared these off for your things. (*She goes over to the window.*) The best part about this room . . . you can look down and see a bit of the street and the canal. There's a houseboat . . . you can see the end of it . . . a bargeman lives there with his family . . . They have a baby and he's just beginning to walk and I'm so afraid he's going to fall into the canal some day. I watch him . . .

Dussel (*Interrupting*). Your father spoke of a schedule.

Anne (*Coming away from the window*). Oh, yes. It's mostly about the times we have to be quiet. And times for the w.c. You can use it now if you like.

Dussel (*Stiffly*). No, thank you.

Anne. I suppose you think it's awful, my talking about a thing like that. But you don't know how important it can get to be, especially when you're frightened . . . About this room, the way Margot and I did . . . she had it to herself in the afternoons for studying, reading . . . lessons, you know . . . and I took the mornings. Would that be all right with you?

Dussel. I'm not at my best in the morning.

Anne. You stay here in the mornings then. I'll take the room in the afternoons.

Dussel. Tell me, when you're in here, what happens to me? Where am I spending my time? In there, with all the people?

Anne. Yes.

Dussel. I see. I see.

Anne. We have supper at half past six.

Dussel (*Going over to the sofa*). Then, if you don't mind . . . I like to lie down quietly for ten minutes before eating. I find it helps the digestion.

Anne. Of course. I hope I'm not going to be too much of a bother to you. I seem to be able to get everyone's back up.

(Dussel *lies down on the sofa, curled up, his back to her.*)

Dussel. I always get along very well with children. My patients all bring their children to me, because they know I get on well with them. So don't you worry about that.

(Anne *leans over him, taking his hand and shaking it gratefully.*)

Anne. Thank you. Thank you, Mr. Dussel.

(The lights dim to darkness. The curtain falls on the scene. Anne's voice comes to us faintly at first, and then with increasing power.)

Anne's Voice. . . . And yesterday I finished Cissy Van Marxvelt's latest book. I think she is a first-class writer. I shall definitely let my children read her. Monday the twenty-first of September, nineteen forty-two. Mr. Dussel and I had another battle yesterday. Yes, Mr. Dussel! According to him, nothing, I repeat . . . nothing, is right about me . . . my appearance, my character, my manners. While he was going on at me I thought . . . sometime I'll give you such a smack that you'll fly right up to the ceiling! Why is it that every grownup thinks he knows the way to bring up children? Particularly the grownups that never had any. I keep wishing that Peter was a girl instead of a boy. Then I would have someone to talk to. Margot's a darling, but she takes everything too seriously. To pause for a moment on the subject of Mrs. Van Daan. I must tell you that her attempts to flirt with father are getting her nowhere. Pim, thank goodness, won't play.

(As she is saying the last lines, the curtain rises on the darkened scene. Anne's voice fades out.)

Scene IV

It is the middle of the night, several months later. The stage is dark except for a little light which comes through the skylight in Peter's room.

Everyone is in bed. Mr. and Mrs. Frank lie on the couch in the main room, which has been pulled out to serve as a makeshift double bed.

Margot is sleeping on a mattress on the floor in the main room, behind a curtain stretched across for privacy. The others are all in their accustomed rooms.

From outside we hear two drunken soldiers singing "Lili Marlene." A girl's high giggle is heard. The sound of running feet is heard coming closer and then fading in the distance. Throughout the scene there is the distant sound of airplanes passing overhead.

A match suddenly flares up in the attic. We dimly see Mr. Van Daan. He is getting his bearings. He comes quickly down the stairs, and goes to the cupboard where the food is stored. Again the match flares up, and is as quickly blown out. The dim figure is seen to steal back up the stairs.

There is quiet for a second or two, broken only by the sound of airplanes, and running feet on the street below.

Suddenly, out of the silence and the dark, we hear Anne scream.

Anne (*Screaming*). No! No! Don't . . . don't take me!

(*She moans, tossing and crying in her sleep. The other people wake, terrified. Dussel sits up in bed, furious.*)

Dussel. Shush! Anne! Anne, for God's sake, shush!

Anne (*Still in her nightmare*). Save me! Save me!

(*She screams and screams.* Dussel *gets out of bed, going over to her, trying to wake her.*)

Dussel. For God's sake! Quiet! Quiet! You want someone to hear?

(*In the main room* Mrs. Frank *grabs a shawl and pulls it around her. She rushes in to* Anne, *taking her in her arms.* Mr. Frank *hurriedly gets up, putting on his overcoat.* Margot *sits up, terrified.* Peter's *light goes on in his room.*)

Mrs. Frank (*To* Anne, *in her room*). Hush, darling, hush. It's all right. It's all right. (*Over her shoulder to* Dussel) Will you be kind enough to turn on the light, Mr. Dussel? (*Back to* Anne) It's nothing, my darling. It was just a dream.

(Dussel *turns on the light in the bedroom.* Mrs. Frank *holds* Anne *in her arms. Gradually* Anne *comes out of her night-mare, still trembling with horror.* Mr. Frank *comes into the room, and goes quickly to the window, looking out to be sure that no one outside had heard* Anne's *screams.* Mrs. Frank *holds* Anne, *talking softly to her. In the main room* Margot *stands on a chair, turning on the center hanging lamp. A light goes on in the* Van Daans' *room overhead.* Peter *puts his robe on, coming out of his room.*)

Dussel (*To* Mrs. Frank, *blowing his nose*). Something must be done about that child, Mrs. Frank. Yelling like that! Who knows but there's somebody on the streets? She's endangering all our lives.

Mrs. Frank. Anne, darling.

Dussel. Every night she twists and turns. I don't sleep. I spend half my night shushing her. And now it's nightmares!

(Margot *comes to the door of* Anne's *room, followed by* Peter. Mr. Frank *goes to them, indicating that everything is all right.* Peter *takes* Margot *back.*)

Mrs. Frank (*To* Anne). You're here, safe, you see? Nothing has happened. (*To* Dussel) Please, Mr. Dussel, go back to bed. She'll be herself in a minute or two. Won't you, Anne?

Dussel (*Picking up a book and a pillow*). Thank you, but I'm going to the w.c. The one place where there's peace! (*He stalks out. Mr. Van Daan, in underwear and trousers, comes down the stairs.*)

Mr. Van Daan (*To* Dussel). What is it? What happened?

Dussel. A nightmare. She was having a nightmare!

Mr. Van Daan. I thought someone was murdering her.

Dussel. Unfortunately, no.—has

(*He goes into the bathroom. Mr. Van Daan goes back up the stairs. Mr. Frank, in the main room, sends Peter back to his own bedroom.*)

Mr. Frank. Thank you, Peter. Go back to bed.

(*Peter goes back to his room. Mr. Frank follows him, turning out the light and looking out the window. Then he goes back to the main room, and gets up on a chair, turning out the center hanging lamp.*)

Mrs. Frank (*To* Anne). Would you like some water? (*Anne shakes her head.*) Was it a very bad dream? Perhaps if you told me . . . ?

Anne. I'd rather not talk about it.

Mrs. Frank. Poor darling. Try to sleep then. I'll sit right here beside you until you fall asleep. (*She brings a stool over, sitting there.*)

Anne. You don't have to.

Mrs. Frank. But I'd like to stay with you . . . very much. Really.

Anne. I'd rather you didn't.

Mrs. Frank. Good night, then. (*She leans down to kiss* Anne. Anne *throws her arm up over her face, turning away.* Mrs. Frank, *hiding her hurt, kisses* Anne's arm.) You'll be all right? There's nothing that you want?

Anne. Will you please ask Father to come.

Mrs. Frank (*After a second*). Of course, Anne dear. (*She hurries out into the other room.* Mr. Frank *comes to her as she comes in*) *Sie verlangt nach Dir!*

Mr. Frank (*Sensing her hurt*). Edith, *Liebe, schau . . .*

Mrs. Frank. *Es macht nichts! Ich danke dem lieben Herrgott, dass sie sich wenigstens an Dich wendet, wenn sie Trost braucht! Geh hinein, Otto, sie ist ganz hysterisch vor Angst.* (*As* Mr. Frank *hesitates*) *Geh zu ihr.* (*He looks at her for a second and then goes to get a cup of water for* Anne. Mrs. Frank *sinks down on the bed, her face in her hands, trying to keep from sobbing aloud.* Margot *comes over to her, putting her arms around her.*) She wants nothing of me. She pulled away when I leaned down to kiss her.

Margot. It's a phase . . . You heard Father . . . Most girls go through it . . . they turn to their fathers at this age . . . they give all their love to their fathers.

Mrs. Frank. You weren't like this. You didn't shut me out.

Margot. She'll get over it . . . (*She smooths the bed for* Mrs. Frank *and sits beside her a moment as* Mrs. Frank *lies down. In* Anne's *room* Mr. Frank *comes in, sitting down by* Anne. Anne *flings her arms around him, clinging to him. In the distance we hear the sound of ack-ack.*)

Anne. Oh, Pim. I dreamed that they came to get us! The Green Police! They broke down the door and grabbed me and started to drag me out the way they did Jopie.

Mr. Frank. I want you to take this pill.

Anne. What is it?

Mr. Frank. Something to quiet you.

(*She takes it and drinks the water. In the main room* Margot *turns out the light and goes back to her bed.*)

Mr. Frank (*To* Anne). Do you want me to read to you for a while?

Anne. No. Just sit with me for a minute. Was I awful? Did I yell terribly loud? Do you think anyone outside could have heard?

Mr. Frank. No. No. Lie quietly now. Try to sleep.

Anne. I'm a terrible coward. I'm so disappointed in myself. I think I've conquered my fear . . . I think I'm really grown-up . . . and then something happens . . . and I run to you like a baby . . . I love you, Father. I don't love anyone but you.

Mr. Frank (*Reproachfully*). Annele!

Anne. It's true. I've been thinking about it for a long time. You're the only one I love.

Mr. Frank. It's fine to hear you tell me that you love me. But I'd be happier if you said you loved your mother as well . . . She needs your help so much . . . your love . . .

Anne. We have nothing in common. She doesn't understand me. Whenever I try to explain my views on life to her she asks me if I'm constipated.

Mr. Frank. You hurt her very much just now. She's crying. She's in there crying.

Anne. I can't help it. I only told the truth. I didn't want her here . . . (*Then, with sudden change*) Oh, Pim, I was horrible, wasn't I? And the worst of it is, I can stand off and look at myself doing it and know it's cruel and yet I can't stop doing it. What's the matter with me? Tell me. Don't say it's just a phase! Help me.

Mr. Frank. There is so little that we parents can do to help our children. We can only try to set a good example . . . point the way. The rest you must do yourself. You must build your own character.

Anne. I'm trying. Really I am. Every night I think back over all of the things I did that day that were wrong . . . like putting the wet mop in Mr. Dussel's bed . . . and this thing now with Mother. I say to myself, that was wrong. I make up my mind, I'm never going to do that again. Never! Of course I may do something worse . . . but at least I'll never do that again! . . . I have a nicer side, Father . . . a sweeter, nicer side. But I'm scared to show it. I'm afraid that people are going to laugh at me if I'm serious. So the mean Anne comes to the outside and the good Anne stays on the inside, and I keep on trying to switch them around and have the good Anne outside and the bad Anne inside and be what I'd like to be . . . and might be . . . if only . . . only . . . (*She is asleep.* Mr. Frank *watches her for a moment and then turns off the light, and starts out. The lights dim out. The curtain falls on the scene. Anne's voice is heard dimly at first, and then with growing strength.*)

Anne's Voice. . . . The air raids are getting worse. They come over day and night. The noise is terrifying.

Pim says it should be music to our ears. The more planes, the sooner will come the end of the war. Mrs. Van Daan pretends to be a fatalist. What will be, will be. But when the planes come over, who is the most frightened? No one else but Petronella! . . . Monday, the ninth of November, nineteen forty-two. Wonderful news! The Allies have landed in Africa. Pim says that we can look for an early finish to the war. Just for fun he asked each of us what was the first thing we wanted to do when we got out of here. Mrs. Van Daan longs to be home with her own things, her needle-point chairs, the Beckstein piano her father gave her . . . the best that money could buy. Peter would like to go to a movie. Mr. Dussel wants to get back to his dentist's drill. He's afraid he is losing his touch. For myself, there are so many things . . . to ride a bike again . . . to laugh till my belly aches . . . to have new clothes from the skin out . . . to have a hot tub filled to overflowing and wallow in it for hours . . . to be back in school with my friends . . .

(*As the last lines are being said, the curtain rises on the scene. The lights dim on as Anne's voice fades away.*)

Scene V

It is the first night of the Hanukkah celebration. Mr. Frank is standing at the head of the table on which is the Menorah. He lights the Shamos, or servant candle, and holds it as he says the blessing. Seated listening is all of the "family," dressed in their best. The men wear hats, Peter *wears his cap.*

Mr. Frank (*Reading from a prayer book*). "Praised be Thou, oh Lord our God, Ruler of the universe, who has sanctified us with Thy commandments and bidden us kindle the Hanukkah lights. Praised be Thou, oh Lord our God, Ruler of the universe, who has wrought wondrous deliverances for our fathers in days of old. Praised be Thou, oh Lord our God, Ruler of the universe, that Thou has given us life and sustenance and brought us to this happy season." (Mr. Frank *lights the one candle of the Menorah as he continues.*) "We kindle this Hanukkah light to celebrate the great and wonderful deeds wrought through the zeal with which God filled the hearts of the heroic Maccabees, two thousand years ago. They fought against indifference, against tyranny and oppression, and they restored our Temple to us. May these lights remind us that we should ever look to God, whence cometh our help." Amen. [*Pronounced* O-mayn.]

All. Amen.

(Mr. Frank *hands* Mrs. Frank *the prayer book.*)

Mrs. Frank (*Reading*). "I lift up mine eyes unto the mountains, from whence cometh my help. My help cometh from the Lord who made heaven and earth. He will not suffer thy foot to be moved. He that keepeth thee will not slumber. He that keepeth Israel doth neither slumber nor sleep. The Lord is thy keeper. The Lord is thy shade upon thy right hand. The sun shall not smite thee by day, nor the moon by night. The Lord shall keep thee from all evil. He shall keep thy soul. The Lord shall guard thy going out and thy coming in, from this time forth and forevermore." Amen.

All. Amen.

(Mrs. Frank *puts down the prayer book and goes to get the food and wine.* Margot *helps her.* Mr. Frank *takes the men's hats and puts them aside.*)

Dussel (*Rising*). That was very moving.

Anne (*Pulling him back*). It isn't over yet!

Mrs. Van Daan. Sit down! Sit down!

Anne. There's a lot more, songs and presents.

Dussel. Presents?

Mrs. Frank. Not this year, unfortunately.

Mrs. Van Daan. But always on Hanukkah everyone gives presents . . . everyone!

Dussel. Like our St. Nicholas' Day. (*There is a chorus of "no's" from the group.*)

Mrs. Van Daan. No! Not like St. Nicholas! What kind of a Jew are you that you don't know Hanukkah?

Mrs. Frank (*As she brings the food*). I remember particularly the candles . . . First one, as we have tonight. Then the second night you light two candles, the next night three . . . and so on until you have eight candles burning. When there are eight candles it is truly beautiful.

Mrs. Van Daan. And the potato pancakes.

Mr. Van Daan. Don't talk about them!

Mrs. Van Daan. I make the best latkes you ever tasted!

Mrs. Frank. Invite us all next year . . . in your own home.

Mr. Frank. God willing!

Mrs. Van Daan. God willing.

Margot. What I remember best is the presents we used to get when we were little . . . eight days of presents . . . and each day they got better and better.

Mrs. Frank (*Sitting down*). We are all here, alive. That is present enough.

Anne. No, it isn't. I've got something . . . (*She rushes into her room, hurriedly puts on a little hat improvised from the lamp shade, grabs a satchel bulging with parcels and comes running back.*)

Mrs. Frank. What is it?

Anne. Presents!

Mrs. Van Daan. Presents!

Dussel. Look!

Mr. Van Daan. What's she got on her head?

Peter. A lamp shade!

Anne (*She picks out one at random.*). This is for Margot. (*She hands it to* Margot, *pulling her to her feet.*) Read it out loud.

Margot (*Reading*).
"You have never lost your temper.
You never will, I fear,

You are so good.
But if you should,
 Put all your cross words here."
(*She tears open the package.*)
A new crossword puzzle book! Where did you
get it?

Anne. It isn't new. It's one that you've done. But I
rubbed it all out, and if you wait a little and forget,
you can do it all over again.

Margot (*Sitting*). It's wonderful, Anne. Thank you.
You'd never know it wasn't new.

(*From outside we hear the sound of a streetcar passing.*)

Anne (*With another gift*). Mrs. Van Daan.

Mrs. Van Daan (*Taking it*). This is awful . . . I haven't
anything for anyone . . . I never thought . . .

Mr. Frank. This is all Anne's idea.

Mrs. Van Daan (*Holding up a bottle*). What is it?

Anne. It's hair shampoo. I took all the odds and ends
of soap and mixed them with the last of my toilet
water.

Mrs. Van Daan. Oh, Anneke!

Anne. I wanted to write a poem for all of them, but I
didn't have time. (*Offering a large box to* Mr. Van Daan)
Yours, Mr. Van Daan, is really something . . .
something you want more than anything. (*As she
waits for him to open it*) Look! Cigarettes!

Mr. Van Daan. Cigarettes!

Anne. Two of them! Pim found some old pipe
tobacco in the pocket lining of his coat . . . and we
made them . . . or rather, Pim did.

Mrs. Van Daan. Let me see . . . Well, look at that! Light it, Putti! Light it.

(Mr. Van Daan *hesitates.*)

Anne. It's tobacco, really it is! There's a little fluff in it, but not much.

(*Everyone watches intently as* Mr. Van Daan *cautiously lights it. The cigarette flares up. Everyone laughs.*)

Peter. It works!

Mrs. Van Daan. Look at him.

Mr. Van Daan (*Spluttering*). Thank you, Anne. Thank you.

(Anne *rushes back to her satchel for another present.*)

Anne (*Handing her mother a piece of paper*). For Mother, Hanukkah greeting. (*She pulls her mother to her feet.*)

Mrs. Frank (*She reads*). "Here's an I.O.U. that I promise to pay.
Ten hours of doing whatever you say. Signed, Anne Frank." (Mrs. Frank, *touched, takes Anne in her arms, holding her close.*)

Dussel (*To* Anne). Ten hours of doing what you're told? Anything you're told?

Anne. That's right.

Dussel. You wouldn't want to sell that, Mrs. Frank?

Mrs. Frank. Never! This is the most precious gift I've ever had! (*She sits, showing her present to the others.* Anne *hurries back to the satchel and pulls out a scarf, the scarf that* Mr. Frank *found in the first scene.*)

Anne (*Offering it to her father*). For Pim.

Mr. Frank. Anneke . . . I wasn't supposed to have a

present! (*He takes it, unfolding it and showing it to the others.*)

Anne. It's a muffler . . . to put round your neck . . . like an ascot, you know. I made it myself out of odds and ends . . . I knitted it in the dark each night, after I'd gone to bed. I'm afraid it looks better in the dark!

Mr. Frank (*Putting it on*). It's fine. It fits me perfectly. Thank you, Annele.

(Anne *hands* Peter *a ball of paper, with a string attached to it.*)

Anne. That's for Mouschi.

Peter (*Rising to bow*). On behalf of Mouschi, I thank you.

Anne (*Hesitant, handing him a gift*). And . . . this is yours . . . from Mrs. Quack Quack. (*As he holds it gingerly in his hands*) Well . . . open it . . . Aren't you going to open it?

Peter. I'm scared to. I know something's going to jump out and hit me.

Anne. No. It's nothing like that, really.

Mrs. Van Daan (*As he is opening it*). What is it, Peter? Go on. Show it.

Anne (*Excitedly*). It's a safety razor!

Dussel. A what?

Anne. A razor!

Mrs. Van Daan (*Looking at it*). You didn't make that out of odds and ends.

Anne (*To Peter*). Miep got it for me. It's not new. It's second-hand. But you really do need a razor now.

Dussel. For what?

Anne. Look on his upper lip . . . you can see the beginning of a mustache.

Dussel. He wants to get rid of that? Put a little milk on it and let the cat lick it off.

Peter (*Starting for his room*). Think you're funny, don't you.

Dussel. Look! He can't wait! He's going in to try it!

Peter. I'm going to give Mouschi his present! (*He goes to his room, slamming the door behind him.*)

Mr. Van Daan (*Disgustedly*). Mouschi, Mouschi, Mouschi.

(*In the distance we hear a dog persistently barking.* Anne *brings a gift to* Dussel.)

Anne. And last but never least, my roommate, Mr. Dussel.

Dussel. For me? You have something for me? (*He opens the small box she gives him.*)

Anne. I made them myself.

Dussel (*Puzzled*). Capsules! Two capsules!

Anne. They're ear-plugs!

Dussel. Ear-plugs?

Anne. To put in your ears so you won't hear me when I thrash around at night. I saw them advertised in a magazine. They're not real ones . . . I made them out of cotton and candle wax. Try them . . . See if they don't work . . . see if you can hear me talk . . .

Dussel (*Putting them in his ears*). Wait now until I get them in . . . so.

Anne. Are you ready?

Dussel. Huh?

Anne. Are you ready?

Dussel. Good God! They've gone inside! I can't get them out! (*They laugh as* Mr. Dussel *jumps about, trying to shake the plugs out of his ears. Finally he gets them out. Putting them away.*) Thank you, Anne! Thank you!

Together.

> **Mr. Van Daan.** A real Hanukkah!
>
> **Mrs. Van Daan.** Wasn't it cute of her?
>
> **Mrs. Frank.** I don't know when she did it.
>
> **Margot.** I love my present.

Anne (*Sitting at the table*). And now let's have the song, Father . . . please . . . (*To* Dussel) Have you heard the Hanukkah song, Mr. Dussel? The song is the whole thing! (*She sings*) "Oh, Hanukkah! Oh Hanukkah! The sweet celebration . . ."

Mr. Frank (*Quieting her*). I'm afraid, Anne, we shouldn't sing that song tonight. (*To* Dussel) It's a song of jubilation, of rejoicing. One is apt to become too enthusiastic.

Anne. Oh, please, please. Let's sing the song. I promise not to shout!

Mr. Frank. Very well. But quietly now . . . I'll keep an eye on you and when . . .

(*As* Anne *starts to sing, she is interrupted by* Dussel, *who is snorting and wheezing.*)

Dussel (*Pointing to* Peter). You . . . You! (Peter *is coming* *from his bedroom, ostentatiously holding a bulge in his coat as if he were holding his cat, and dangling* Anne's *present before it.*) How many times . . . I told you . . . Out! Out!

Mr. Van Daan (*Going to* Peter). What's the matter with you? Haven't you any sense? Get that cat out of here.

Peter (*Innocently*). Cat?

Mr. Van Daan. You heard me. Get it out of here!

Peter. I have no cat. (*Delighted with his joke, he opens his coat and pulls out a bath towel. The group at the table laugh, enjoying the joke.*)

Dussel (*Still wheezing*). It doesn't need to be the cat . . . his clothes are enough . . . when he comes out of that room . . .

Mr. Van Daan. Don't worry. You won't be bothered any more. We're getting rid of it.

Dussel. At last you listen to me. (*He goes off into his bedroom.*)

Mr. Van Daan (*Calling after him*). I'm not doing it for you. That's all in your mind . . . all of it! (*He starts back to his place at the table.*) I'm doing it because I'm sick of seeing that cat eat all our food.

Peter. That's not true! I only give him bones . . . scraps . . .

Mr. Van Daan. Don't tell me! He gets fatter every day! Damn cat looks better than any of us. Out he goes tonight!

Peter. No! No!

Anne. Mr. Van Daan, you can't do that! That's Peter's cat. Peter loves that cat.

Mrs. Frank (*Quietly*). Anne.

Peter (*To* Mr. Van Daan). If he goes, I go.

Mr. Van Daan. Go! Go!

Mrs. Van Daan. You're not going and the cat's not going! Now please . . . this is Hanukkah . . . Hanukkah . . . this is the time to celebrate . . . What's the matter with all of you? Come on, Anne. Let's have the song.

Anne (*Singing*). "Oh, Hanukkah! Oh, Hanukkah! The sweet celebration."

Mr. Frank (*Rising*). I think we should first blow out the candle . . . then we'll have something for tomorrow night.

Margot. But, Father, you're supposed to let it burn itself out.

Mr. Frank. I'm sure that God understands shortages. (*Before blowing it out*) "Praised be Thou, oh Lord our God, who hast sustained us and permitted us to celebrate this joyous festival."

(*He is about to blow out the candle when suddenly there is a crash of something falling below. They all freeze in horror, motionless. For a few seconds there is complete silence. Mr. Frank slips off his shoes. The others noiselessly follow his example. Mr. Frank turns out a light near him. He motions to Peter to turn off the center lamp. Peter tries to reach it, realizes he cannot and gets up on a chair. Just as he is touching the lamp he loses his balance. The chair goes out from under him. He falls. The iron lamp shade crashes to the floor. There is a sound of feet below, running down the stairs.*)

Mr. Van Daan (*Under his breath*). God Almighty! (*The only light left comes from the Hanukkah candle. Dussel* comes from his room. Mr. Frank *creeps over to the stairwell and stands listening. The dog is heard barking excitedly.*) Do you hear anything?

Mr. Frank (*In a whisper*). No. I think they've gone.

Mrs. Van Daan. It's the Green Police. They've found us.

Mr. Frank. If they had, they wouldn't have left. They'd be up here by now.

Mrs. Van Daan. I know it's the Green Police. They've gone to get help. That's all. They'll be back!

Mr. Van Daan. Or it may have been the Gestapo, looking for papers . . .

Mr. Frank (*Interrupting*). Or a thief, looking for money.

Mrs. Van Daan. We've got to do something . . . Quick! Quick! Before they come back.

Mr. Van Daan. There isn't anything to do. Just wait.

(Mr. Frank *holds up his hand for them to be quiet. He is listening intently. There is complete silence as they all strain to hear any sound from below. Suddenly* Anne *begins to sway. With a low cry she falls to the floor in a faint. Mrs. Frank goes to her quickly, sitting beside her on the floor and taking her in her arms.*)

Mrs. Frank. Get some water, please! Get some water!

(Margot *starts for the sink.*)

Mr. Van Daan (*Grabbing* Margot). No! No! No one's going to run water!

Mr. Frank. If they've found us, they've found us. Get the water. (Margot *starts again for the sink.* Mr. Frank, *getting a flashlight*) I'm going down.

(Margot *rushes to him, clinging to him.* Anne *struggles to consciousness.*)

Margot. No, Father, no! There may be someone there, waiting . . . It may be a trap!

Mr. Frank. This is Saturday. There is no way for us to know what has happened until Miep or Mr. Kraler comes on Monday morning. We cannot live with this uncertainty.

Margot. Don't go, Father!

Mrs. Frank. Hush, darling, hush. (Mr. Frank *slips quietly out, down the steps and out through the door below.*) Margot! Stay close to me.

(Margot *goes to her mother.*)

Mr. Van Daan. Shush! Shush!

(Mrs. Frank *whispers to* Margot *to get the water.* Margot *goes for it.*)

Mrs. Van Daan. Putti, where's our money? Get our money. I hear you can buy the Green Police off, so much a head. Go upstairs quick! Get the money!

Mr. Van Daan. Keep still!

Mrs. Van Daan (*Kneeling before him, pleading*). Do you want to be dragged off to a concentration camp? Are you going to stand there and wait for them to come up and get you? Do something, I tell you!

Mr. Van Daan (*Pushing her aside*). Will you keep still! (He *goes over to the stairwell to listen.* Peter *goes to his mother, helping her up onto the sofa. There is a second of silence, then* Anne *can stand it no longer.*)

Anne. Someone go after Father! Make Father come back!

Peter (*Starting for the door*). I'll go.

Mr. Van Daan. Haven't you done enough? (*He pushes Peter roughly away. In his anger against his father Peter grabs a chair as if to hit him with it, then puts it down, burying his face in his hands. Mrs. Frank begins to pray softly.*)

Anne. Please, please, Mr. Van Daan. Get Father.

Mr. Van Daan. Quiet! Quiet!

(*Anne is shocked into silence. Mrs. Frank pulls her closer, holding her protectively in her arms.*)

Mrs. Frank (*Softly, praying*). "I lift up mine eyes unto the mountains, from whence cometh my help. My help cometh from the Lord who made heaven and earth. He will not suffer thy foot to be moved . . . He that keepeth thee will not slumber . . ." (*She stops as she hears someone coming. They all watch the door tensely. Mr. Frank comes quietly in. Anne rushes to him, holding him tight.*)

Mr. Frank. It was a thief. That noise must have scared him away.

Mrs. Van Daan. Thank God.

Mr. Frank. He took the cash box. And the radio. He ran away in such a hurry that he didn't stop to shut the street door. It was swinging wide open. (*A breath of relief sweeps over them*) I think it would be good to have some light.

Margot. Are you sure it's all right?

Mr. Frank. The danger has passed. (*Margot goes to light the small lamp.*) Don't be so terrified, Anne. We're safe.

Dussel. Who says the danger has passed? Don't you realize we are in greater danger than ever?

Mr. Frank. Mr. Dussel, will you be still!

(Mr. Frank *takes* Anne *back to the table, making her sit down with him, trying to calm her.*)

Dussel (*Pointing to* Peter). Thanks to this clumsy fool, there's someone now who knows we're up here! Someone now knows we're up here, hiding!

Mrs. Van Daan (*Going to* Dussel). Someone knows we're here, yes. But who is the someone? A thief! A thief! You think a thief is going to go to the Green Police and say . . . I was robbing a place the other night and I heard a noise up over my head? You think a thief is going to do that?

Dussel. Yes. I think he will.

Mrs. Van Daan (*Hysterically*). You're crazy! (*She stumbles back to her seat at the table.* Peter *follows protectively, pushing* Dussel *aside.*)

Dussel. I think some day he'll be caught and then he'll make a bargain with the Green Police . . . if they'll let him off, he'll tell them where some Jews are hiding! (*He goes off into the bedroom. There is a second of appalled silence.*)

Mr. Van Daan. He's right.

Anne. Father, let's get out of here! We can't stay here now . . . Let's go . . .

Mr. Van Daan. Go! Where?

Mrs. Frank (*Sinking into her chair at the table*). Yes. Where?

Mr. Frank (*Rising, to them all*). Have we lost all faith? All courage? A moment ago we thought that they'd come for us. We were sure it was the end. But it wasn't the end. We're alive, safe. (Mr. Van Daan *goes to the table and sits.* Mr. Frank *prays.*) "We thank Thee, oh Lord our God, that in Thy infinite mercy Thou hast again seen fit to spare us." (*He blows out the candle, then turns to* Anne) Come on, Anne. The song! Let's have the song! (*He starts to sing.* Anne *finally starts falteringly to sing, as* Mr. Frank *urges her on. Her voice is hardly audible at first.*)

Anne (*Singing*). "Oh, Hanukkah! Oh, Hanukkah! The sweet . . . celebration . . ." (*As she goes on singing, the others gradually join in, their voices still shaking with fear.* Mrs. Van Daan *sobs as she sings.*)

Group. "Around the feast . . . we . . . gather
In complete . . . jubilation . . .
Happiest of sea . . . sons
Now is here.
Many are the reasons for good cheer."

(Dussel *comes from the bedroom. He comes over to the table, standing beside* Margot, *listening to them as they sing.*)

"Together
We'll weather
Whatever tomorrow may bring."

(*As they sing on with growing courage, the lights start to dim.*)

"So hear us rejoicing
And merrily voicing
The Hanukkah song that we sing.
Hoy!"

(The lights are out. The curtain starts slowly to fall.)

"Hear us rejoicing
And merrily voicing
The Hanukkah song that we sing."

(They are still singing, as the curtain falls.)

Curtain

Act Two

....

Scene I

In the darkness we hear Anne's *voice, again reading from the diary.*

Anne's Voice. Saturday, the first of January, nineteen forty-four. Another new year has begun and we find ourselves still in our hiding place. We have been here now for one year, five months and twenty-five days. It seems that our life is at a standstill.

The curtain rises on the scene. It is late afternoon. Everyone is bundled up against the cold. In the main room Mrs. Frank is taking down the laundry which is hung across the back. Mr. Frank sits in the chair down left, reading. Margot *is lying on the couch with a blanket over her and the many-colored knitted scarf around her throat.* Anne *is seated at the center table, writing in her diary.* Peter, Mr. *and* Mrs. Van Daan *and* Dussel *are all in their own rooms, reading or lying down.*

As the lights dim on, Anne's *voice continues, without a break.*

Anne's Voice. We are all a little thinner. The Van Daans' "discussions" are as violent as ever. Mother still does not understand me. But then I don't understand her either. There is one great change, however. A change in myself. I read somewhere that girls of my age don't feel quite certain of themselves. That they become quiet within and begin to think of the miracle that is taking place in their bodies. I think that what is happening to me is so wonderful . . . not only what can be seen, but what is taking place inside. Each time it has happened I have a feeling that I have a sweet secret. (*We hear the chimes and then a hymn being played on the carillon outside.*) And in spite of any pain, I long for the time when I shall feel that secret within me again.

(*The buzzer of the door below suddenly sounds. Everyone is startled,* Mr. Frank *tiptoes cautiously to the top of the steps and listens. Again the buzzer sounds, in* Miep's *V-for-Victory signal.*)

Mr. Frank. It's Miep! (*He goes quickly down the steps to unbolt the door.* Mrs. Frank *calls upstairs to the* Van Daans *and then to* Peter.)

Mrs. Frank. Wake up, everyone! Miep is here! (Anne *quickly puts her diary away.* Margot *sits up, pulling the blanket around her shoulders.* Mr. Dussel *sits on the edge of his bed, listening, disgruntled.* Miep *comes up the steps, followed by* Mr. Kraler. *They bring flowers, books, newspapers, etc.* Anne *rushes to* Miep, *throwing her arms affectionately around her.*) Miep . . . and Mr. Kraler . . . What a delightful surprise!

Mr. Kraler. We came to bring you New Year's greetings.

Mrs. Frank. You shouldn't . . . you should have at least one day to yourselves. (*She goes quickly to the stove and brings down teacups and tea for all of them.*)

Anne. Don't say that, it's so wonderful to see them! (*Sniffing at* Miep's *coat*) I can smell the wind and the cold on your clothes.

Miep (*Giving her the flowers*). There you are. (*Then to* Margot, *feeling her forehead*) How are you, Margot? . . . Feeling any better?

Margot. I'm all right.

Anne. We filled her full of every kind of pill so she won't cough and make a noise. (*She runs into her room to put the flowers in water. Mr. and Mrs. Van Daan come from upstairs. Outside there is the sound of a band playing.*)

Mrs. Van Daan. Well, hello, Miep. Mr. Kraler.

Mr. Kraler (*Giving a bouquet of flowers to* Mrs. Van Daan). With my hope for peace in the New Year.

Peter (*Anxiously*). Miep, have you seen Mouschi? Have you seen him anywhere around?

Miep. I'm sorry, Peter. I asked everyone in the neighborhood had they seen a gray cat. But they said no.

(Mrs. Frank *gives* Miep *a cup of tea.* Mr. Frank *comes up the steps, carrying a small cake on a plate.*)

Mr. Frank. Look what Miep's brought for us!

Mrs. Frank (*Taking it*). A cake!

Mr. Van Daan. A cake! (*He pinches* Miep's *cheeks gaily and hurries up to the cupboard.*) I'll get some plates.

(Dussel, *in his room, hastily puts a coat on and starts out to join the others.*)

Mrs. Frank. Thank you, Miepia. You shouldn't have done it. You must have used all of your sugar ration for weeks. (*Giving it to* Mrs. Van Daan) It's beautiful, isn't it?

Mrs. Van Daan. It's been ages since I even saw a cake.

Not since you brought us one last year. (*Without looking at the cake, to* Miep) Remember? Don't you remember, you gave us one on New Year's Day? Just this time last year? I'll never forget it because you had "Peace in nineteen forty-three" on it. (*She looks at the cake and reads.*) "Peace in nineteen forty-four!"

Miep. Well, it has to come sometime, you know. (*As* Dussel *comes from his room*) Hello, Mr. Dussel.

Mr. Kraler. How are you?

Mr. Van Daan (*Bringing plates and a knife*). Here's the knife, liefje. Now, how many of us are there?

Miep. None for me, thank you.

Mr. Frank. Oh, please. You must.

Miep. I couldn't.

Mr. Van Daan. Good! That leaves one . . . two . . . three . . . seven of us.

Dussel. Eight! Eight! It's the same number as it always is!

Mr. Van Daan. I left Margot out. I take it for granted Margot won't eat any.

Anne. Why wouldn't she!

Mrs. Frank. I think it won't harm her.

Mr. Van Daan. All right! All right! I just didn't want her to start coughing again, that's all.

Dussel. And please, Mrs. Frank should cut the cake.

Together.

 Mr. Van Daan. What's the difference?

Mrs. Van Daan. It's not Mrs. Frank's cake, is it, Miep? It's for all of us.

Dussel. Mrs. Frank divides things better.

Together.

Mrs. Van Daan (*Going to* Dussel). What are you trying to say?

Mr. Van Daan. Oh, come on! Stop wasting time!

Mrs. Van Daan (*To* Dussel). Don't I always give everybody exactly the same? Don't I?

Mr. Van Daan. Forget it, Kerli.

Mrs. Van Daan. No. I want an answer! Don't I?

Dussel. Yes. Yes. Everybody gets exactly the same . . . except Mr. Van Daan always gets a little bit more.

(Van Daan *advances on* Dussel, *the knife still in his hand*)

Mr. Van Daan. That's a lie!

(Dussel *retreats before the onslaught of the* Van Daans.)

Mr. Frank. Please, please! (*Then to* Miep) You see what a little sugar cake does to us? It goes right to our heads!

Mr. Van Daan (*Handing* Mrs. Frank *the knife*). Here you are, Mrs. Frank.

Mrs. Frank. Thank you. (*Then to* Miep *as she goes to the table to cut the cake*) Are you sure you won't have some?

Miep (*Drinking her tea*). No, really, I have to go in a minute.

(*The sound of the band fades out in the distance.*)

Peter (*To* Miep). Maybe Mouschi went back to our

house . . . they say that cats . . . Do you ever get over there . . . ? I mean . . . do you suppose you could . . . ?

Miep. I'll try, Peter. The first minute I get I'll try. But I'm afraid, with him gone a week . . .

Dussel. Make up your mind, already someone has had a nice big dinner from that cat!

(Peter *is furious, inarticulate. He starts toward* Dussel *as if to hit him.* Mr. Frank *stops him.* Mrs. Frank *speaks quickly to ease the situation.*)

Mrs. Frank (*To* Miep). This is delicious, Miep!

Mrs. Van Daan (*Eating hers*). Delicious!

Mr. Van Daan (*Finishing it in one gulp*). Dirk's in luck to get a girl who can bake like this!

Miep (*Putting down her empty teacup*). I have to run. Dirk's taking me to a party tonight.

Anne. How heavenly! Remember now what everyone is wearing, and what you have to eat and everything, so you can tell us tomorrow.

Miep. I'll give you a full report! Good-bye, everyone!

Mr. Van Daan (*To* Miep). Just a minute. There's something I'd like you to do for me. (*He hurries off up the stairs to his room.*)

Mrs. Van Daan (*Sharply*). Putti, where are you going? (*She rushes up the stairs after him, calling hysterically*) What do you want? Putti, what are you going to do?

Miep (*To* Peter). What's wrong?

Peter (*His sympathy is with his mother*). Father says he's going to sell her fur coat. She's crazy about that old fur coat.

Dussel. Is it possible? Is it possible that anyone is so silly as to worry about a fur coat in times like this?

Peter. It's none of your darn business . . . and if you say one more thing . . . I'll, I'll take you and I'll . . . I mean it . . . I'll . . .

(*There is a piercing scream from* Mrs. Van Daan *above. She grabs at the fur coat as* Mr. Van Daan *is starting downstairs with it.*)

Mrs. Van Daan. No! No! No! Don't you dare take that! You hear? It's mine! (*Downstairs* Peter *turns away, embarrassed, miserable.*) My father gave me that! You didn't give it to me. You have no right. Let go of it . . . you hear?

(Mr. Van Daan *pulls the coat from her hands and hurries downstairs.* Mrs. Van Daan *sinks to the floor, sobbing. As* Mr. Van Daan *comes into the main room the others look away, embarrassed for him.*)

Mr. Van Daan (*To* Mr. Kraler). Just a little—discussion over the advisability of selling this coat. As I have often reminded Mrs. Van Daan, it's very selfish of her to keep it when people outside are in such desperate need of clothing . . . (*He gives the coat to* Miep.) So if you will please to sell it for us? It should fetch a good price. And by the way, will you get me cigarettes. I don't care what kind they are . . . get all you can.

Miep. It's terribly difficult to get them, Mr. Van Daan. But I'll try. Good-bye.

(*She goes.* Mr. Frank *follows her down the steps to bolt the door after her.* Mrs. Frank *gives* Mr. Kraler *a cup of tea.*)

Mrs. Frank. Are you sure you won't have some cake, Mr. Kraler?

Mr. Kraler. I'd better not.

Mr. Van Daan. You're still feeling badly? What does your doctor say?

Mr. Kraler. I haven't been to him.

Mrs. Frank. Now, Mr. Kraler! . . .

Mr. Kraler (*Sitting at the table*). Oh, I tried. But you can't get near a doctor these days . . . they're so busy. After weeks I finally managed to get one on the telephone. I told him I'd like an appointment . . . I wasn't feeling very well. You know what he answers . . . over the telephone . . . Stick out your tongue! (*They laugh. He turns to* Mr. Frank *as* Mr. Frank *comes back*) I have some contracts here . . . I wonder if you'd look over them with me . . .

Mr. Frank (*Putting out his hand*). Of course.

Mr. Kraler (*He rises*). If we could go downstairs . . . (Mr. Frank *starts ahead*, Mr. Kraler *speaks to the others*) Will you forgive us? I won't keep him but a minute. (*He starts to follow* Mr. Frank *down the steps.*)

Margot (*With sudden foreboding*). What's happened? Something's happened! Hasn't it, Mr. Kraler?

(Mr. Kraler *stops and comes back, trying to reassure* Margot *with a pretense of casualness.*)

Mr. Kraler. No, really. I want your father's advice . . .

Margot. Something's gone wrong! I know it!

Mr. Frank (*Coming back, to* Mr. Kraler). If it's something that concerns us here, it's better that we all hear it.

Mr. Kraler (*Turning to him, quietly*). But . . . the children . . . ?

Mr. Frank. What they'd imagine would be worse than any reality.

(*As* Mr. Kraler *speaks, they all listen with intense apprehension.* Mrs. Van Daan *comes down the stairs and sits on the bottom step.*)

Mr. Kraler. It's a man in the storeroom . . . I don't know whether or not you remember him . . . Carl, about fifty, heavy-set, near-sighted . . . He came with us just before you left.

Mr. Frank. He was from Utrecht?

Mr. Kraler. That's the man. A couple of weeks ago, when I was in the storeroom, he closed the door and asked me . . . how's Mr. Frank? What do you hear from Mr. Frank? I told him I only knew there was a rumor that you were in Switzerland. He said he'd heard that rumor too, but he thought I might know something more. I didn't pay any attention to it . . . but then a thing happened yesterday . . . He'd brought some invoices to the office for me to sign. As I was going through them, I looked up. He was standing staring at the bookcase . . . your bookcase. He said he thought he remembered a door there . . . Wasn't there a door there that used to go up to the loft? Then he told me he wanted more money. Twenty guilders more a week.

Mr. Van Daan. Blackmail!

Mr. Frank. Twenty guilders? Very modest blackmail.

Mr. Van Daan. That's just the beginning.

Dussel (*Coming to* Mr. Frank). You know what I think? He was the thief who was down there that night.

That's how he knows we're here.

Mr. Frank (*To* Mr. Kraler). How was it left? What did you tell him?

Mr. Kraler. I said I had to think about it. What shall I do? Pay him the money? . . . Take a chance on firing him . . . or what? I don't know.

Dussel (*Frantic*). For God's sake don't fire him! Pay him what he asks . . . keep him here where you can have your eye on him.

Mr. Frank. Is it so much that he's asking? What are they paying nowadays?

Mr. Kraler. He could get it in a war plant. But this isn't a war plant. Mind you, I don't know if he really knows . . . or if he doesn't know.

Mr. Frank. Offer him half. Then we'll soon find out if it's blackmail or not.

Dussel. And if it is? We've got to pay it, haven't we? Anything he asks we've got to pay!

Mr. Frank. Let's decide that when the time comes.

Mr. Kraler. This may be all my imagination. You get to a point, these days, where you suspect everyone and everything. Again and again . . . on some simple look or word, I've found myself . . .

(*The telephone rings in the office below.*)

Mrs. Van Daan (*Hurrying to* Mr. Kraler). There's the telephone! What does that mean, the telephone ringing on a holiday?

Mr. Kraler. That's my wife. I told her I had to go over some papers in my office . . . to call me there when she got out of church. (*He starts out.*) I'll offer him half then. Good-bye . . . we'll hope for the best!

(*The group call their good-bye's half-heartedly. Mr. Frank follows Mr. Kraler, to bolt the door below. During the following scene, Mr. Frank comes back up and stands listening, disturbed.*)

Dussel (*To Mr. Van Daan*). You can thank your son for this . . . smashing the light! I tell you, it's just a question of time now. (*He goes to the window at the back and stands looking out.*)

Margot. Sometimes I wish the end would come . . . whatever it is.

Mrs. Frank (*Shocked*). Margot!

(*Anne goes to Margot, sitting beside her on the couch with her arms around her.*)

Margot. Then at least we'd know where we were.

Mrs. Frank. You should be ashamed of yourself! Talking that way! Think how lucky we are! Think of the thousands dying in the war, every day. Think of the people in concentration camps.

Anne (*Interrupting*). What's the good of that? What's the good of thinking of misery when you're already miserable? That's stupid!

Mrs. Frank. Anne!

(*As Anne goes on raging at her mother, Mrs. Frank tries to break in, in an effort to quiet her.*)

Anne. We're young, Margot and Peter and I! You grownups have had your chance! But look at us . . . If we begin thinking of all the horror in the world, we're lost! We're trying to hold onto some kind of ideals . . . when everything . . . ideals, hopes . . . everything, are being destroyed! It isn't our fault that the world is in such a mess! We weren't around when all this started! So don't try to take it out on us!

(*She rushes off to her room, slamming the door after her. She picks up a brush from the chest and hurls it to the floor. Then she sits on the settee, trying to control her anger.*)

Mr. Van Daan. She talks as if we started the war! Did we start the war? (*He spots* Anne's *cake. As he starts to take it,* Peter *anticipates him.*)

Peter. She left her cake. (*He starts for* Anne's *room with the cake. There is silence in the main room. Mrs. Van Daan goes up to her room, followed by Van Daan. Dussel stays looking out the window. Mr. Frank brings Mrs. Frank her cake. She eats it slowly, without relish. Mr. Frank takes his cake to Margot and sits quietly on the sofa beside her. Peter stands in the doorway of Anne's darkened room, looking at her, then makes a little movement to let her know he is there. Anne sits up, quickly, trying to hide the signs of her tears. Peter holds out the cake to her.*) You left this.

Anne (*Dully*). Thanks.

(Peter *starts to go out, then comes back.*)

Peter. I thought you were fine just now. You know just how to talk to them. You know just how to say it. I'm no good . . . I never can think . . . especially when I'm mad . . . That Dussel . . . when he said that about Mouschi . . . someone eating him . . . all I could think is . . . I wanted to hit him. I wanted to give him such a . . . a . . . that he'd . . . That's what I used to do when there was an argument at school . . . That's the way I . . . but here . . . And an old man like that . . . it wouldn't be so good.

Anne. You're making a big mistake about me. I do it

all wrong. I say too much. I go too far. I hurt people's feelings . . .

(Dussel *leaves the window, going to his room.*)

Peter. I think you're just fine . . . What I want to say . . . if it wasn't for you around here, I don't know. What I mean . . .

(Peter *is interrupted by* Dussel's *turning on the light. Dussel stands in the doorway, startled to see* Peter. Peter *advances toward him forbiddingly.* Dussel *backs out of the room.* Peter *closes the door on him.*)

Anne. Do you mean it, Peter? Do you really mean it?

Peter. I said it, didn't I?

Anne. Thank you, Peter!

(*In the main room* Mr. *and* Mrs. Frank *collect the dishes and take them to the sink, washing them.* Margot *lies down again on the couch.* Dussel, *lost, wanders into* Peter's *room and takes up a book, starting to read.*)

Peter (*Looking at the photographs on the wall*). You've got quite a collection.

Anne. Wouldn't you like some in your room? I could give you some. Heaven knows you spend enough time in there . . . doing heaven knows what . . .

Peter. It's easier. A fight starts, or an argument . . . I duck in there.

Anne. You're lucky, having a room to go to. His lordship is always here . . . I hardly ever get a minute alone. When they start in on me, I can't duck away. I have to stand there and take it.

Peter. You gave some of it back just now.

Anne. I get so mad. They've formed their opinions

. . . about everything . . . but we . . . we're still trying to find out . . . We have problems here that no other people our age have ever had. And just as you think you've solved them, something comes along and bang! You have to start all over again.

Peter. At least you've got someone you can talk to.

Anne. Not really. Mother . . . I never discuss anything serious with her. She doesn't understand. Father's all right. We can talk about everything . . . everything but one thing. Mother. He simply won't talk about her. I don't think you can be really intimate with anyone if he holds something back, do you?

Peter. I think your father's fine.

Anne. Oh, he is, Peter! He is! He's the only one who's ever given me the feeling that I have any sense. But anyway, nothing can take the place of school and play and friends of your own age . . . or near your age . . . can it?

Peter. I suppose you miss your friends and all.

Anne. It isn't just . . . (*She breaks off, staring up at him for a second*) Isn't it funny, you and I? Here we've been seeing each other every minute for almost a year and a half, and this is the first time we've ever really talked. It helps a lot to have someone to talk to, don't you think? It helps you to let off steam.

Peter (*Going to the door*). Well, any time you want to let off steam, you can come into my room.

Anne (*Following him*). I can get up an awful lot of steam. You'll have to be careful how you say that.

Peter. It's all right with me.

Anne. Do you mean it?

Peter. I said it, didn't I?

(*He goes out. Anne stands in her doorway looking after him. As* Peter *gets to his door he stands for a minute looking back at her. Then he goes into his room.* Dussel *rises as he comes in, and quickly passes him, going out. He starts across for his room.* Anne *sees him coming, and pulls her door shut.* Dussel *turns back toward* Peter's *room.*

Peter *pulls his door shut.* Dussel *stands there, bewildered, forlorn.*

The scene slowly dims out. The curtain falls on the scene. Anne's *voice comes over in the darkness . . . faintly at first, and then with growing strength.*)

Anne's Voice. We've had bad news. The people from whom Miep got our ration books have been arrested. So we have had to cut down on our food. Our stomachs are so empty that they rumble and make strange noises, all in different keys. Mr. Van Daan's is deep and low, like a bass fiddle. Mine is high, whistling like a flute. As we all sit around waiting for supper, it's like an orchestra tuning up. It only needs Toscanini to raise his baton and we'd be off in the Ride of the Valkyries. Monday, the sixth of March, nineteen forty-four. Mr. Kraler is in the hospital. It seems he has ulcers. Pim says we are his ulcers. Miep has to run the business and us too. The Americans have landed on the southern tip of Italy. Father looks for a quick finish to the war. Mr. Dussel is waiting every day for the warehouse man to demand more money. Have I been skipping too much from one subject to another? I can't help it. I feel that spring is coming. I feel it in my whole body and soul. I feel utterly confused. I am longing . . . so longing . . . for everything . . . for friends . . . for someone to talk to . . . someone who understands . . . someone young, who feels as I do . . .

(*As these last lines are being said, the curtain rises on the scene. The lights dim on. Anne's voice fades out.*)

Scene II

It is evening, after supper. From outside we hear the sound of children playing. The "grownups," with the exception of Mr. Van Daan, are all in the main room. Mrs. Frank is doing some mending, Mrs. Van Daan is reading a fashion magazine. Mr. Frank is going over business accounts. Dussel, in his dentist's jacket, is pacing up and down, impatient to get into his bedroom. Mr. Van Daan is upstairs working on a piece of embroidery in an embroidery frame.

In his room Peter is sitting before the mirror, smoothing his hair. As the scene goes on, he puts on his tie, brushes his coat and puts it on, preparing himself meticulously for a visit from Anne. On his wall are now hung some of Anne's motion picture stars.

In her room Anne too is getting dressed. She stands before the mirror in her slip, trying various ways of dressing her hair. Margot is seated on the sofa, hemming a skirt for Anne to wear.

In the main room Dussel can stand it no longer. He comes over, rapping sharply on the door of his and Anne's bedroom.

Anne (*Calling to him*). No, no, Mr. Dussel! I am not dressed yet. (*Dussel walks away, furious, sitting down and burying his head in his hands. Anne turns to Margot.*) How is that? How does that look?

Margot (*Glancing at her briefly*). Fine.

Anne. You didn't even look.

Margot. Of course I did. It's fine.

Anne. Margot, tell me, am I terribly ugly?

Margot. Oh, stop fishing.

Anne. No. No. Tell me.

Margot. Of course you're not. You've got nice eyes . . . and a lot of animation, and . . .

Anne. A little vague, aren't you?

(*She reaches over and takes a brassière out of* Margot's *sewing basket. She holds it up to herself, studying the effect in the mirror. Outside,* Mrs. Frank, *feeling sorry for* Dussel, *comes over, knocking at the girls' door.*)

Mrs. Frank (*Outside*). May I come in?

Margot. Come in, Mother.

Mrs. Frank (*Shutting the door behind her*). Dr. Dussel's impatient to get in here.

Anne (*Still with the brassière*). Heavens, he takes the room for himself the entire day.

Mrs. Frank (*Gently*). Anne, dear, you're not going in again tonight to see Peter?

Anne (*Dignified*). That is my intention.

Mrs. Frank. But you've already spent a great deal of time in there today.

Anne. I was in there exactly twice. Once to get the dictionary, and then three-quarters of an hour before supper.

Mrs. Frank. Aren't you afraid you're disturbing him?

Anne. Mother, I have some intuition.

Mrs. Frank. Then may I ask you this much, Anne. Please don't shut the door when you go in.

Anne. You sound like Mrs. Van Daan! (*She throws the brassière back in* Margot's *sewing basket and picks up her blouse, putting it on.*)

Mrs. Frank. No. No. I don't mean to suggest anything wrong. I only wish that you wouldn't expose yourself to criticism . . . that you wouldn't give Mrs. Van Daan the opportunity to be unpleasant.

Anne. Mrs. Van Daan doesn't need an opportunity to be unpleasant!

Mrs. Frank. Everyone's on edge, worried about Mr. Kraler. This is one more thing . . .

Anne. I'm sorry, Mother. I'm going to Peter's room. I'm not going to let Petronella Van Daan spoil our friendship.

(Mrs. Frank *hesitates for a second, then goes out, closing the door after her. She gets a pack of playing cards and sits at the center table, playing solitaire. In* Anne's *room* Margot *hands the finished skirt to* Anne. *As* Anne *is putting it on,* Margot *takes off her high-heeled shoes and stuffs paper in the toes so that* Anne *can wear them.*)

Margot (*To* Anne). Why don't you two talk in the main room? It'd save a lot of trouble. It's hard on Mother, having to listen to those remarks from Mrs. Van Daan and not say a word.

Anne. Why doesn't she say a word? I think it's ridiculous to take it and take it.

Margot. You don't understand Mother at all, do you? She can't talk back. She's not like you. It's just not in her nature to fight back.

Anne. Anyway . . . the only one I worry about is you. I feel awfully guilty about you. (*She sits on the stool near* Margot, *putting on* Margot's *high-heeled shoes.*)

Margot. What about?

Anne. I mean, every time I go into Peter's room, I

have a feeling I may be hurting you. (Margot *shakes her head.*) I know if it were me, I'd be wild. I'd be desperately jealous, if it were me.

Margot. Well, I'm not.

Anne. You don't feel badly? Really? Truly? You're not jealous?

Margot. Of course I'm jealous . . . jealous that you've got something to get up in the morning for . . . But jealous of you and Peter? No.

(Anne *goes back to the mirror.*)

Anne. Maybe there's nothing to be jealous of. Maybe he doesn't really like me. Maybe I'm just taking the place of his cat . . . (*She picks up a pair of short white gloves, putting them on.*) Wouldn't you like to come in with us?

Margot. I have a book.

(*The sound of the children playing outside fades out. In the main room* Dussel *can stand it no longer. He jumps up, going to the bedroom door and knocking sharply.*)

Dussel. Will you please let me in my room!

Anne. Just a minute, dear, dear Mr. Dussel. (*She picks up her Mother's pink stole and adjusts it elegantly over her shoulders, then gives a last look in the mirror.*) Well, here I go . . . to run the gauntlet. (*She starts out, followed by* Margot.)

Dussel (*As she appears—sarcastic*). Thank you so much.

(Dussel *goes into his room.* Anne *goes toward* Peter's *room, passing* Mrs. Van Daan *and her parents at the center table.*)

Mrs. Van Daan. My God, look at her! (Anne *pays no attention. She knocks at* Peter's *door.*) I don't know what good it is to have a son. I never see him. He wouldn't care if I killed myself. (Peter *opens the door and stands aside for* Anne *to come in.*) Just a minute, Anne. (*She goes to them at the door.*) I'd like to say a few words to my son. Do you mind? (Peter *and* Anne *stand waiting.*) Peter, I don't want you staying up till all hours tonight. You've got to have your sleep. You're a growing boy. You hear?

Mrs. Frank. Anne won't stay late. She's going to bed promptly at nine. Aren't you, Anne?

Anne. Yes, Mother . . . (*To* Mrs. Van Daan) May we go now?

Mrs. Van Daan. Are you asking me? I didn't know I had anything to say about it.

Mrs. Frank. Listen for the chimes, Anne dear.

(*The two young people go off into* Peter's *room, shutting the door after them.*)

Mrs. Van Daan (*To* Mrs. Frank). In my day it was the boys who called on the girls. Not the girls on the boys.

Mrs. Frank. You know how young people like to feel that they have secrets. Peter's room is the only place where they can talk.

Mrs. Van Daan. Talk! That's not what they called it when I was young.

(Mrs. Van Daan *goes off to the bathroom.* Margot *settles down to read her book.* Mr. Frank *puts his papers away and brings a chess game to the center table. He and* Mrs. Frank *start to play. In* Peter's *room,* Anne *speaks to* Peter, *indignant, humiliated.*)

Anne. Aren't they awful? Aren't they impossible? Treating us as if we were still in the nursery.

(*She sits on the cot.* Peter *gets a bottle of pop and two glasses.*)

Peter. Don't let it bother you. It doesn't bother me.

Anne. I suppose you can't really blame them . . . they think back to what *they* were like at our age. They don't realize how much more advanced we are . . . When you think what wonderful discussions we've had! . . . Oh, I forgot. I was going to bring you some more pictures.

Peter. Oh, these are fine, thanks.

Anne. Don't you want some more? Miep just brought me some new ones.

Peter. Maybe later. (*He gives her a glass of pop and, taking some for himself, sits down facing her.*)

Anne (*Looking up at one of the photographs*). I remember when I got that . . . I won it. I bet Jopie that I could eat five ice-cream cones. We'd all been playing ping-pong . . . We used to have heavenly times . . . we'd finish up with ice cream at the Delphi, or the Oasis, where Jews were allowed . . . there'd always be a lot of boys . . . we'd laugh and joke . . . I'd like to go back to it for a few days or a week. But after that I know I'd be bored to death. I think more seriously about life now. I want to be a journalist . . . or something. I love to write. What do you want to do?

Peter. I thought I might go off some place . . . work on a farm or something . . . some job that doesn't take much brains.

Anne. You shouldn't talk that way. You've got the most awful inferiority complex.

Peter. I know I'm not smart.

Anne. That isn't true. You're much better than I am in dozens of things . . . arithmetic and algebra and . . . well, you're a million times better than I am in algebra. (*With sudden directness*) You like Margot, don't you? Right from the start you liked her, liked her much better than me.

Peter (*Uncomfortably*). Oh, I don't know.

(*In the main room* Mrs. Van Daan *comes from the bathroom and goes over to the sink, polishing a coffee pot.*)

Anne. It's all right. Everyone feels that way. Margot's so good. She's sweet and bright and beautiful and I'm not.

Peter. I wouldn't say that.

Anne. Oh, no, I'm not. I know that. I know quite well that I'm not a beauty. I never have been and never shall be.

Peter. I don't agree at all. I think you're pretty.

Anne. That's not true!

Peter. And another thing. You've changed . . . from at first, I mean.

Anne. I have?

Peter. I used to think you were awful noisy.

Anne. And what do you think now, Peter? How have I changed?

Peter. Well . . . er . . . you're . . . quieter.

(*In his room* Dussel *takes his pajamas and toilet articles and goes into the bathroom to change.*)

Anne. I'm glad you don't just hate me.

Peter. I never said that.

Anne. I bet when you get out of here you'll never think of me again.

Peter. That's crazy.

Anne. When you get back with all of your friends, you're going to say . . . now what did I ever see in that Mrs. Quack Quack.

Peter. I haven't got any friends.

Anne. Oh, Peter, of course you have. Everyone has friends.

Peter. Not me. I don't want any. I get along all right without them.

Anne. Does that mean you can get along without me? I think of myself as your friend.

Peter. No. If they were all like you, it'd be different.

(*He takes the glasses and the bottle and puts them away. There is a second's silence and then* Anne *speaks, hesitantly, shyly.*)

Anne. Peter, did you ever kiss a girl?

Peter. Yes. Once.

Anne (*To cover her feelings*). That picture's crooked. (Peter *goes over, straightening the photograph.*) Was she pretty?

Peter. Huh?

Anne. The girl that you kissed.

Peter. I don't know. I was blindfolded. (*He comes back and sits down again.*) It was at a party. One of those kissing games.

Anne (*Relieved*). Oh. I don't suppose that really counts, does it?

Peter. It didn't with me.

Anne. I've been kissed twice. Once a man I'd never seen before kissed me on the cheek when he picked me up off the ice and I was crying. And the other was Mr. Koophuis, a friend of Father's who kissed my hand. You wouldn't say those counted, would you?

Peter. I wouldn't say so.

Anne. I know almost for certain that Margot would never kiss anyone unless she was engaged to them. And I'm sure too that Mother never touched a man before Pim. But I don't know . . . things are so different now . . . What do you think? Do you think a girl shouldn't kiss anyone except if she's engaged or something? It's so hard to try to think what to do, when here we are with the whole world falling around our ears and you think . . . well . . . you don't know what's going to happen tomorrow and . . . What do you think?

Peter. I suppose it'd depend on the girl. Some girls, anything they do's wrong. But others . . . well . . . it wouldn't necessarily be wrong with them. (*The carillon starts to strike nine o'clock.*) I've always thought that when two people . . .

Anne. Nine o'clock. I have to go.

Peter. That's right.

Anne (*Without moving*). Good night.

(*There is a second's pause, then* Peter *gets up and moves toward the door.*)

Peter. You won't let them stop you coming?

Anne. No. (*She rises and starts for the door*) Sometime I might bring my diary. There are so many things in it that I want to talk over with you. There's a lot about you.

Peter. What kind of thing?

Anne. I wouldn't want you to see some of it. I thought you were a nothing, just the way you thought about me.

Peter. Did you change your mind, the way I changed my mind about you?

Anne. Well . . . You'll see . . .

(*For a second* Anne *stands looking up at* Peter, *longing for him to kiss her. As he makes no move she turns away. Then suddenly* Peter *grabs her awkwardly in his arms, kissing her on the cheek.* Anne *walks out dazed. She stands for a minute, her back to the people in the main room. As she regains her poise she goes to her mother and father and* Margot, *silently kissing them. They murmur their good nights to her. As she is about to open her bedroom door, she catches sight of* Mrs. Van Daan. *She goes quickly to her, taking her face in her hands and kissing her first on one cheek and then on the other. Then she hurries off into her room.* Mrs. Van Daan *looks after her, and then looks over at* Peter's *room. Her suspicions are confirmed.*)

Mrs. Van Daan (*She knows*). Ah hah!

(*The lights dim out. The curtain falls on the scene. In the darkness* Anne's *voice comes faintly at first and then with growing strength.*)

Anne's Voice. By this time we all know each other so well that if anyone starts to tell a story, the rest can finish it for him. We're having to cut down still further on our meals. What makes it worse, the rats have been at work again. They've carried off some of our precious food. Even Mr. Dussel wishes now that Mouschi was here. Thursday, the twentieth of April, nineteen forty-four. Invasion fever is mounting every day. Miep tells us that people outside talk of nothing else. For myself, life has become much more pleasant. I often go to Peter's room after supper. Oh, don't think I'm in love, because I'm not. But it does make life more bearable to have someone with whom you can exchange views. No more tonight. P.S. . . . I must be honest. I must confess that I actually live for the next meeting. Is there anything lovelier than to sit under the skylight and feel the sun on your cheeks and have a darling boy in your arms? I admit now that I'm glad the Van Daans had a son and not a daughter. I've outgrown another dress. That's the third. I'm having to wear Margot's clothes after all. I'm working hard on my French and am now reading *La Belle Nivernaise*.

(*As she is saying the last lines—the curtain rises on the scene. The lights dim on, as* Anne's *voice fades out.*)

Scene III

It is night, a few weeks later. Everyone is in bed. There is complete quiet. In the Van Daans' *room a match flares up for a moment and then is quickly put out. Mr. Van Daan, in bare feet, dressed in underwear and trousers, is dimly seen coming stealthily down the stairs and into the main room, where Mr. and Mrs. Frank and Margot are sleeping. He goes to the food safe and again lights a match. Then he cautiously opens the safe, taking out a half-loaf of bread. As he closes the safe, it creaks. He stands rigid. Mrs. Frank sits up in bed. She sees him.*

Mrs. Frank (*Screaming*). Otto! Otto! *Komme schnell!*

(*The rest of the people wake, hurriedly getting up.*)

Mr. Frank. *Was ist los? Was ist passiert?*

(Dussel, *followed by* Anne, *comes from his room.*)

Mrs. Frank (*As she rushes over to* Mr. Van Daan). *Er stiehlt das Essen!*

Dussel (*Grabbing* Mr. Van Daan). You! You! Give me that.

Mrs. Van Daan (*Coming down the stairs*). Putti . . . Putti . . . what is it?

Dussel (*His hands on* Van Daan's *neck*). You dirty thief . . . stealing food . . . you good-for-nothing . . .

Mr. Frank. Mr. Dussel! For God's sake! Help me, Peter!

(Peter *comes over, trying, with* Mr. Frank, *to separate the two struggling men.*)

Peter. Let him go! Let go!

(Dussel *drops* Mr. Van Daan, *pushing him away. He shows*

them the end of a loaf of bread that he has taken from Van
Daan.)

Dussel. You greedy, selfish . . . !

(Margot *turns on the lights.*)

Mrs. Van Daan. Putti . . . what is it?

(*All of* Mrs. Frank's *gentleness, her self-control, is gone. She
is outraged, in a frenzy of indignation.*)

Mrs. Frank. The bread! He was stealing the bread!

Dussel. It was you, and all the time we thought it was
the rats!

Mr. Frank. Mr. Van Daan, how could you!

Mr. Van Daan. I'm hungry.

Mrs. Frank. We're all of us hungry! I see the children
getting thinner and thinner. Your own son Peter
. . . I've heard him moan in his sleep, he's so
hungry. And you come in the night and steal food
that should go to them . . . to the children!

Mrs. Van Daan (*Going to* Mr. Van Daan *protectively*). He
needs more food than the rest of us. He's used to
more. He's a big man.

(Mr. Van Daan *breaks away, going over and sitting on the
couch.*)

Mrs. Frank (*Turning on* Mrs. Van Daan). And you . . .
you're worse than he is! You're a mother, and yet
you sacrifice your child to this man . . . this . . . this
. . .

Mr. Frank. Edith! Edith!

(Margot *picks up the pink woolen stole, putting it over her
mother's shoulders.*)

Mrs. Frank (*Paying no attention, going on to* Mrs. Van Daan). Don't think I haven't seen you! Always saving the choicest bits for him! I've watched you day after day and I've held my tongue. But not any longer! Not after this! Now I want him to go! I want him to get out of here!

Together.

Mr. Frank. Edith!

Mr. Van Daan. Get out of here?

Mrs. Van Daan. What do you mean?

Mrs. Frank. Just that! Take your things and get out!

Mr. Frank (*To* Mrs. Frank). You're speaking in anger. You cannot mean what you are saying.

Mrs. Frank. I mean exactly that!

(Mrs. Van Daan *takes a cover from the* Franks' *bed, pulling it about her.*)

Mr. Frank. For two long years we have lived here, side by side. We have respected each other's rights . . . we have managed to live in peace. Are we now going to throw it all away? I know this will never happen again, will it, Mr. Van Daan?

Mr. Van Daan. No. No.

Mrs. Frank. He steals once! He'll steal again!

(Mr. Van Daan, *holding his stomach, starts for the bathroom.* Anne *puts her arms around him, helping him up the step.*)

Mr. Frank. Edith, please. Let us be calm. We'll all go to our rooms . . . and afterwards we'll sit down quietly and talk this out . . . we'll find some way . . .

Mrs. Frank. No! No! No more talk! I want them to leave!

Mrs. Van Daan. You'd put us out, on the streets?

Mrs. Frank. There are other hiding places.

Mrs. Van Daan. A cellar . . . a closet. I know. And we have no money left even to pay for that.

Mrs. Frank. I'll give you money. Out of my own pocket I'll give it gladly. (*She gets her purse from a shelf and comes back with it.*)

Mrs. Van Daan. Mr. Frank, you told Putti you'd never forget what he'd done for you when you came to Amsterdam. You said you could never repay him, that you . . .

Mrs. Frank (*Counting out money*). If my husband had any obligation to you, he's paid it, over and over.

Mr. Frank. Edith, I've never seen you like this before. I don't know you.

Mrs. Frank. I should have spoken out long ago.

Dussel. You can't be nice to some people.

Mrs. Van Daan (*Turning on* Dussel). There would have been plenty for all of us, if you hadn't come in here!

Mr. Frank. We don't need the Nazis to destroy us. We're destroying ourselves.

(*He sits down, with his head in his hands.* Mrs. Frank *goes to* Mrs. Van Daan.)

Mrs. Frank (*Giving* Mrs. Van Daan *some money*). Give this to Miep. She'll find you a place.

Anne. Mother, you're not putting *Peter* out. Peter hasn't done anything.

Mrs. Frank. He'll stay, of course. When I say I must protect the children, I mean Peter too.

(Peter *rises from the steps where he has been sitting.*)

Peter. I'd have to go if Father goes.

(Mr. Van Daan *comes from the bathroom. Mrs. Van Daan hurries to him and takes him to the couch. Then she gets water from the sink to bathe his face.*)

Mrs. Frank (*While this is going on*). He's no father to you . . . that man! He doesn't know what it is to be a father!

Peter (*Starting for his room*). I wouldn't feel right. I couldn't stay.

Mrs. Frank. Very well, then. I'm sorry.

Anne (*Rushing over to* Peter). No, Peter! No! (Peter *goes into his room, closing the door after him.* Anne *turns back to her mother, crying.*) I don't care about the food. They can have mine! I don't want it! Only don't send them away. It'll be daylight soon. They'll be caught . . .

Margot (*Putting her arms comfortingly around* Anne). Please, Mother!

Mrs. Frank. They're not going now. They'll stay here until Miep finds them a place. (*To* Mrs. Van Daan) But one thing I insist on! He must never come down here again! He must never come to this room where the food is stored! We'll divide what we have . . . an equal share for each! (Dussel *hurries over to get a sack of potatoes from the food safe. Mrs. Frank goes on, to* Mrs. Van Daan.) You can cook it here and take it up to him.

(Dussel *brings the sack of potatoes back to the center table.*)

Margot. Oh, no. No. We haven't sunk so far that we're going to fight over a handful of rotten potatoes.

Dussel (*Dividing the potatoes into piles*). Mrs. Frank, Mr. Frank, Margot, Anne, Peter, Mrs. Van Daan, Mr. Van Daan, myself . . . Mrs. Frank . . .

(*The buzzer sounds in* Miep's *signal.*)

Mr. Frank. It's Miep! (*He hurries over, getting his overcoat and putting it on.*)

Margot. At this hour?

Mrs. Frank. It is trouble.

Mr. Frank (*As he starts down to unbolt the door*). I beg you, don't let her see a thing like this!

Mr. Dussel (*Counting without stopping*). . . . Anne, Peter, Mrs. Van Daan, Mr. Van Daan, myself . . .

Margot (*To* Dussel). Stop it! Stop it!

Dussel. . . . Mr. Frank, Margot, Anne, Peter, Mrs. Van Daan, Mr. Van Daan, myself, Mrs. Frank . . .

Mrs. Van Daan. You're keeping the big ones for yourself! All the big ones . . . Look at the size of that! . . . And that! . . .

(Dussel *continues on with his dividing.* Peter, *with his shirt and trousers on, comes from his room.*)

Margot. Stop it! Stop it!

(*We hear* Miep's *excited voice speaking to* Mr. Frank *below.*)

Miep. Mr. Frank . . . the most wonderful news! . . . The invasion has begun!

Mr. Frank. Go on, tell them! Tell them!

(Miep *comes running up the steps, ahead of* Mr. Frank. *She has a man's raincoat on over her nightclothes and a bunch of orange-colored flowers in her hand.*)

Miep. Did you hear that, everybody? Did you hear what I said? The invasion has begun! The invasion!

(*They all stare at* Miep, *unable to grasp what she is telling them.* Peter *is the first to recover his wits.*)

Peter. Where?

Mrs. Van Daan. When? When, Miep?

Miep. It began early this morning . . .

(*As she talks on, the realization of what she has said begins to dawn on them. Everyone goes crazy. A wild demonstration takes place.* Mrs. Frank *hugs* Mr. Van Daan.)

Mrs. Frank. Oh, Mr. Van Daan, did you hear that?

(Dussel *embraces* Mrs. Van Daan. Peter *grabs a frying pan and parades around the room, beating on it, singing the Dutch National Anthem.* Anne *and* Margot *follow him, singing, weaving in and out among the excited grownups.* Margot *breaks away to take the flowers from* Miep *and distribute them to everyone. While this pandemonium is going on* Mrs. Frank *tries to make herself heard above the excitement.*)

Mrs. Frank (*To* Miep). How do you know?

Miep. The radio . . . The B.B.C.! They said they landed on the coast of Normandy!

Peter. The British?

Miep. British, Americans, French, Dutch, Poles, Norwegians . . . all of them! More than four thousand ships! Churchill spoke, and General Eisenhower! D-Day they call it!

Mr. Frank. Thank God, it's come!

Mrs. Van Daan. At last!

Miep (*Starting out*). I'm going to tell Mr. Kraler. This'll be better than any blood transfusion.

Mr. Frank (*Stopping her*). What part of Normandy did they land, did they say?

Miep. Normandy . . . that's all I know now . . . I'll be up the minute I hear some more! (*She goes hurriedly out.*)

Mr. Frank (*To* Mrs. Frank). What did I tell you? What did I tell you?

(Mrs. Frank *indicates that he has forgotten to bolt the door after* Miep. *He hurries down the steps.* Mr. Van Daan, *sitting on the couch, suddenly breaks into a convulsive sob. Everybody looks at him, bewildered.*)

Mrs. Van Daan (*Hurrying to him*) Putti! Putti! What is it? What happened?

Mr. Van Daan. Please. I'm so ashamed.

(Mr. Frank *comes back up the steps.*)

Dussel. Oh, for God's sake!

Mrs. Van Daan. Don't, Putti.

Margot. It doesn't matter now!

Mr. Frank (*Going to* Mr. Van Daan). Didn't you hear what Miep said? The invasion has come! We're going to be liberated! This is a time to celebrate!

(He embraces Mrs. Frank *and then hurries to the cupboard and gets the cognac and a glass.*)

Mr. Van Daan. To steal bread from children!

Mrs. Frank. We've all done things that we're ashamed of.

Anne. Look at me, the way I've treated Mother . . . so mean and horrid to her.

Mrs. Frank. No, Anneke, no.

(Anne *runs to her mother, putting her arms around her.*)

Anne. Oh, Mother, I was. I was awful.

Mr. Van Daan. Not like me. No one is as bad as me!

Dussel (*To* Mr. Van Daan). Stop it now! Let's be happy!

Mr. Frank (*Giving* Mr. Van Daan *a glass of cognac*). Here! Here! *Schnapps! Locheim!*

(Van Daan *takes the cognac. They all watch him. He gives them a feeble smile.* Anne *puts up her fingers in a V-for-Victory sign. As* Van Daan *gives an answering V-sign, they are startled to hear a loud sob from behind them. It is* Mrs. Frank, *stricken with remorse. She is sitting on the other side of the room.*)

Mrs. Frank (*Through her sobs*). When I think of the terrible things I said . . .

(Mr. Frank, Anne *and* Margot *hurry to her, trying to comfort her.* Mr. Van Daan *brings her his glass of cognac.*)

Mr. Van Daan. No! No! You were right!

Mrs. Frank. That I should speak that way to you! . . . Our friends! . . . Our guests! (*She starts to cry again.*)

Dussel. Stop it, you're spoiling the whole invasion!

(*As they are comforting her, the lights dim out. The curtain falls.*)

Anne's Voice (*Faintly at first and then with growing strength*). We're all in much better spirits these days. There's still excellent news of the invasion. The best part about it is that I have a feeling that friends are coming. Who knows? Maybe I'll be back in school by fall. Ha, ha! The joke is on us! The warehouse man doesn't know a thing and we are paying him all that money! . . . Wednesday, the second of July, nineteen forty-four. The invasion seems temporarily to be bogged down. Mr. Kraler has to have an operation, which looks bad. The Gestapo have found the radio that was stolen. Mr. Dussel says they'll trace it back and back to the thief, and then, it's just a matter of time till they get to us. Everyone is low. Even poor Pim can't raise their spirits. I have often been downcast myself . . . but never in despair. I can shake off everything if I write. But . . . and that is the great question . . . will I ever be able to write well? I want to so much. I want to go on living even after my death. Another birthday has gone by, so now I am fifteen. Already I know what I want. I have a goal, an opinion.

(As this is being said—the curtain rises on the scene, the lights dim on, and Anne's voice fades out.)

Scene IV

It is an afternoon a few weeks later . . . Everyone but Margot *is in the main room. There is a sense of great tension.*

Both Mrs. Frank *and* Mr. Van Daan *are nervously pacing back and forth,* Dussel *is standing at the window, looking down fixedly at the street below.* Peter *is at the center table, trying to do his lessons.* Anne *sits opposite him, writing in her diary.* Mrs. Van Daan *is seated on the couch, her eyes on* Mr. Frank *as he sits reading.*

The sound of a telephone ringing comes from the office below. They all are rigid, listening tensely. Mr. Dussel *rushes down to* Mr. Frank.

Dussel. There it goes again, the telephone! Mr. Frank, do you hear?

Mr. Frank (*Quietly*). Yes. I hear.

Dussel (*Pleading, insistent*). But this is the third time, Mr. Frank! The third time in quick succession! It's a signal! I tell you it's Miep, trying to get us! For some reason she can't come to us and she's trying to warn us of something!

Mr. Frank. Please. Please.

Mr. Van Daan (*To* Dussel). You're wasting your breath.

Dussel. Something has happened, Mr. Frank. For three days now Miep hasn't been to see us! And today not a man has come to work. There hasn't been a sound in the building!

Mrs. Frank. Perhaps it's Sunday. We may have lost track of the days.

Mr. Van Daan (*To* Anne). You with the diary there. What day is it?

Dussel (*Going to* Mrs. Frank). I don't lose track of the days! I know exactly what day it is! It's Friday, the fourth of August. Friday, and not a man at work. (*He rushes back to* Mr. Frank, *pleading with him, almost in tears.*) I tell you Mr. Kraler's dead. That's the only explanation. He's dead and they've closed down the building, and Miep's trying to tell us!

Mr. Frank. She'd never telephone us.

Dussel (*Frantic*). Mr. Frank, answer that! I beg you, answer it!

Mr. Frank. No.

Mr. Van Daan. Just pick it up and listen. You don't have to speak. Just listen and see if it's Miep.

Dussel (*Speaking at the same time*). For God's sake . . . I ask you.

Mr. Frank. No. I've told you, no. I'll do nothing that might let anyone know we're in the building.

Peter. Mr. Frank's right.

Mr. Van Daan. There's no need to tell us what side you're on.

Mr. Frank. If we wait patiently, quietly, I believe that help will come.

(*There is silence for a minute as they all listen to the telephone ringing.*)

Dussel. I'm going down. (*He rushes down the steps.* Mr. Frank *tries ineffectually to hold him.* Dussel *runs to the lower door, unbolting it. The telephone stops ringing.* Dussel *bolts the door and comes slowly back up the steps.*) Too late. (Mr. Frank *goes to* Margot *in* Anne's *bedroom.*)

Mr. Van Daan. So we just wait here until we die.

Mrs. Van Daan (*Hysterically*). I can't stand it! I'll kill myself! I'll kill myself!

Mr. Van Daan. For God's sake, stop it!

(*In the distance, a German military band is heard playing a Viennese waltz.*)

Mrs. Van Daan. I think you'd be glad if I did! I think you want me to die!

Mr. Van Daan. Whose fault is it we're here? (Mrs. Van Daan *starts for her room. He follows, talking at her.*) We could've been safe somewhere . . . in America or Switzerland. But no! No! You wouldn't leave when I wanted to. You couldn't leave your things. You couldn't leave your precious furniture.

Mrs. Van Daan. Don't touch me!

(*She hurries up the stairs, followed by* Mr. Van Daan. Peter, *unable to bear it, goes to his room.* Anne *looks after him, deeply concerned.* Dussel *returns to his post at the window.* Mr. Frank *comes back into the main room and takes a book, trying to read.* Mrs. Frank *sits near the sink, starting to peel some potatoes.* Anne *quietly goes to* Peter's *room, closing the door after her.* Peter *is lying face down on the cot.* Anne *leans over him, holding him in her arms, trying to bring him out of his despair.*)

Anne. Look, Peter, the sky. (*She looks up through the skylight.*) What a lovely, lovely day! Aren't the clouds beautiful? You know what I do when it seems as if I couldn't stand being cooped up for one more minute? I think myself out. I think myself on a walk in the park where I used to go with Pim. Where the jonquils and the crocus and the violets grow down the slopes. You know the most wonderful part about thinking yourself out? You can have it any way you like. You can have roses and violets and chrysanthemums all blooming at the same time . . . It's funny . . . I used to take it all for granted . . . and now I've gone crazy about everything to do with nature. Haven't you?

Peter. I've just gone crazy. I think if something doesn't happen soon . . . if we don't get out of here . . . I can't stand much more of it!

Anne (*Softly*). I wish you had a religion, Peter.

Peter. No, thanks! Not me!

Anne. Oh, I don't mean you have to be Orthodox . . . or believe in heaven and hell and purgatory and things . . . I just mean some religion . . . it doesn't matter what. Just to believe in something! When I think of all that's out there . . . the trees . . . and flowers . . . and seagulls . . . when I think of the dearness of you, Peter . . . and the goodness of the people we know . . . Mr. Kraler, Miep, Dirk, the vegetable man, all risking their lives for us every day . . . When I think of these good things, I'm not afraid any more . . . I find myself, and God, and I . . .

(Peter *interrupts, getting up and walking away.*)

Peter. That's fine! But when I begin to think, I get mad! Look at us, hiding out for two years. Not able to move! Caught here like . . . waiting for them to come and get us . . . and all for what?

Anne. We're not the only people that've had to suffer. There've always been people that've had to . . . sometimes one race . . . sometimes another . . . and yet . . .

Peter. That doesn't make me feel any better!

Anne (*Going to him*). I know it's terrible, trying to have any faith . . . when people are doing such horrible . . . But you know what I sometimes think? I think the world may be going through a phase, the way I was with Mother. It'll pass, maybe not for hundreds of years, but some day . . . I still believe, in spite of everything, that people are really good at heart.

Peter. I want to see something now . . . Not a thousand years from now! (*He goes over, sitting down again on the cot.*)

Anne. But, Peter, if you'd only look at it as part of a great pattern . . . that we're just a little minute in the life . . . (*She breaks off.*) Listen to us, going at each other like a couple of stupid grownups! Look at the sky now. Isn't it lovely? (*She holds out her hand to him. Peter takes it and rises, standing with her at the window looking out, his arms around her.*) Some day, when we're outside again, I'm going to . . .

(*She breaks off as she hears the sound of a car, its brakes squealing as it comes to a sudden stop. The people in the other rooms also become aware of the sound. They listen tensely. Another car roars up to a screeching stop. Anne and Peter come from Peter's room. Mr. and Mrs. Van Daan creep down the stairs. Dussel comes out from his room. Everyone is listening, hardly breathing. A doorbell clangs again and again in the building below. Mr. Frank starts quietly down the steps to the door. Dussel and Peter follow him. The others stand rigid, waiting, terrified.*

In a few seconds Dussel comes stumbling back up the steps. He shakes off Peter's help and goes to his room. Mr. Frank bolts the door below, and comes slowly back up the steps. Their eyes are all on him as he stands there for a minute. They realize that what they feared has happened.

Mrs. Van Daan *starts to whimper.* Mr. Van Daan *puts her gently in a chair, and then hurries off up the stairs to their room to collect their things. Peter goes to comfort his mother. There is a sound of violent pounding on a door below.*)

Mr. Frank (*Quietly*). For the past two years we have lived in fear. Now we can live in hope.

(*The pounding below becomes more insistent. There are muffled sounds of voices, shouting commands.*)

Men's Voices. *Auf machen! Da drinnen! Auf machen! Schnell! Schnell! Schnell! etc., etc.*

(*The street door below is forced open. We hear the heavy tread of footsteps coming up. Mr. Frank gets two school bags from the shelves, and gives one to Anne and the other to Margot. He goes to get a bag for Mrs. Frank. The sound of feet coming up grows louder. Peter comes to Anne, kissing her good-bye, then he goes to his room to collect his things. The buzzer of their door starts to ring. Mr. Frank brings Mrs. Frank a bag. They stand together, waiting. We hear the thud of gun butts on the door, trying to break it down.*

Anne stands, holding her school satchel, looking over at her father and mother with a soft, reassuring smile. She is no longer a child, but a woman with courage to meet whatever lies ahead.

The lights dim out. The curtain falls on the scene. We hear a mighty crash as the door is shattered. After a second Anne's voice is heard.)

Anne's Voice. And so it seems our stay here is over. They are waiting for us now. They've allowed us five minutes to get our things. We can each take a bag and whatever it will hold of clothing. Nothing else. So, dear Diary, that means I must leave you behind. Good-bye for a while. P.S. Please, please, Miep, or Mr. Kraler, or anyone else. If you should find this diary, will you please keep it safe for me, because some day I hope . . .

(Her voice stops abruptly. There is silence. After a second the curtain rises.)

Scene V

It is again the afternoon in November, 1945. The rooms are as we saw them in the first scene. Mr. Kraler *has joined* Miep *and* Mr. Frank. *There are coffee cups on the table. We see a great change in* Mr. Frank. *He is calm now. His bitterness is gone. He slowly turns a few pages of the diary. They are blank.*

Mr. Frank. No more. (*He closes the diary and puts it down on the couch beside him.*)

Miep. I'd gone to the country to find food. When I got back the block was surrounded by police . . .

Mr. Kraler. We made it our business to learn how they knew. It was the thief . . . the thief who told them.

(Miep *goes up to the gas burner, bringing back a pot of coffee.*)

Mr. Frank (*After a pause*). It seems strange to say this, that anyone could be happy in a concentration camp. But Anne was happy in the camp in Holland where they first took us. After two years of being shut up in these rooms, she could be out . . . out in the sunshine and the fresh air that she loved.

Miep (*Offering the coffee to* Mr. Frank). A little more?

Mr. Frank (*Holding out his cup to her*). The news of the war was good. The British and Americans were sweeping through France. We felt sure that they would get to us in time. In September we were told that we were to be shipped to Poland . . . The men to one camp. The women to another. I was sent to Auschwitz. They went to Belsen. In January we were freed, the few of us who were left. The war wasn't yet over, so it took us a long time to get home. We'd be sent here and there behind the lines where we'd be safe. Each time our train would stop . . . at a siding, or a crossing . . . we'd all get out and go from group to group . . . Where were you? Were you at Belsen? At Buchenwald? At Mauthausen? Is it possible that you knew my wife? Did you ever see my husband? My son? My daughter? That's how I found out about my wife's death . . . of Margot, the Van Daans . . . Dussel. But Anne . . . I still hoped . . . Yesterday I went to Rotterdam. I'd heard of a woman there . . . She'd been in Belsen with Anne . . . I know now.

(*He picks up the diary again, and turns the pages back to find a certain passage. As he finds it we hear* Anne's *voice.*)

Anne's Voice. In spite of everything, I still believe that people are really good at heart.

(Mr. Frank *slowly closes the diary.*)

Mr. Frank. She puts me to shame.

(*They are silent.*)

The Curtain Falls

Related Readings

CONTENTS

from Anne Frank: The Diary of a Young Girl

by Anne Frank

These diary entries will let you hear Anne's own voice. In the first excerpt, written in the early months of hiding, Anne gives us a witty picture of daily life of the seven people gathered in the Secret Annex. As time drags on, Anne uses her diary to explore her hopes, dreams, and deepest thoughts about the meaning of life.

Wednesday, 4 August, 1943

Dear Kitty,

Now that we have been in the "Secret Annexe" for over a year, you know something of our lives, but some of it is quite indescribable. There is so much to tell, everything is so different from ordinary times and from ordinary people's lives. But still, to give you a closer look into our lives, now and again I intend to give you a description of an ordinary day. Today I'm beginning with the evening and night.

Nine o'clock in the evening. The bustle of going to bed in the "Secret Annexe" begins and it is always really quite a business. Chairs are shoved about, beds are pulled down, blankets unfolded, nothing remains where it is during the day. I sleep on the little divan, which is not more than one and a half meters long. So chairs have to be used to lengthen it. A quilt, sheets, pillows, blankets, are all fetched from Dussel's bed where they remain during the day. One hears terrible creaking in the next room: Margot's concertina-bed being pulled out. Again, divan, blankets, and pillows, everything is done to make the wooden slats a bit more comfortable. It sounds like thunder above, but it is only Mrs. Van Daan's bed. This is shifted to the window, you see, in order to give Her Majesty in the pink bed jacket fresh air to tickle her dainty nostrils!

After Peter's finished, I step into the washing cubicle, where I give myself a thorough wash and general toilet; it occasionally happens (only in the hot weeks or months) that there is a tiny flea floating in the water. Then teeth cleaning, hair curling, manicure, and my cotton-wool pads with hydrogen peroxide (to bleach black mustache hairs)—all this in under half an hour.

Half past nine. Quickly into dressing gown, soap in one hand, pottie, hairpins, pants, curlers, and cotton wool in the other, I hurry out of the bathroom; but usually I'm called back once for the various hairs which decorate the washbasin in graceful curves, but which are not approved of by the next person.

Ten o'clock. Put up the blackout. Good night! For at least a quarter of an hour there is creaking of beds and a sighing of broken springs, then all is quiet, at least that is if our neighbors upstairs don't quarrel in bed.

Half past eleven. The bathroom door creaks. A narrow strip of light falls into the room. A squeak of shoes, a large coat, even larger than the man inside it—Dussel returns from his night work in Kraler's office. Shuffling on the floor for ten minutes, crackle of paper (that is the food which has to be stowed away), and a bed is made. Then the form disappears again and one only hears suspicious noises from the lavatory from time to time. . . .

Quarter to seven. Trrrrr—the alarm clock that raises its voice at any hour of the day (if one asks for it and sometimes when one doesn't). Crack—ping— Mrs. Van Daan has turned it off. Creak—Mr. Van Daan gets up. Puts on water and then full speed to the bathroom.

Quarter past seven. The door creaks again. Dussel can go to the bathroom. Once alone, I take down the blackout—and a new day in the "Secret Annexe" has begun.

Yours, Anne

Monday, 9 August, 1943

Dear Kitty,

To continue the "Secret Annexe" daily timetable. I shall now describe the evening meal:

Mr. Van Daan begins. He is first to be served, takes a lot of everything if it is what he likes. Usually talks at the same time, always gives his opinion as the only one worth listening to, and once he has spoken it is irrevocable. Because if anyone *dares* to question it, then he flares up at once. Oh, he can spit like a cat—I'd rather not argue, I can tell you—if you've *once* tried you don't try again. He has the best opinion, he knows the most about everything. All right then, he has got brains, but "self-satisfaction" has reached a high grade with this gentleman.

Madame. Really, I should remain silent. Some

days, especially if there is a bad mood coming on, you can't look at her face. On closer examination, she is the guilty one in all the arguments. Not the subject! Oh, no, everyone prefers to remain aloof over that, but one could perhaps call her the "kindler." Stirring up trouble, that's fun. Mrs. Frank against Anne; Margot against Daddy doesn't go quite so easily.

But now at table, Mrs. Van Daan doesn't go short, although she thinks so at times. The tiniest potatoes, the sweetest mouthful, the best of everything; picking over is her system. The others will get their turn, as long as I have the best. Then talking. Whether anyone is interested, whether they are listening or not, that doesn't seem to matter. I suppose she thinks: "Everyone is interested in what Mrs. Van Daan says." Coquettish smiles, behaving as if one knew everything, giving everyone a bit of advice and encouragement, that's *sure* to make a good impression. But if you look longer, then the good soon wears off.

One, she is industrious, two, gay, three, a coquette—and, occasionally, pretty. This is Petronella Van Daan.

The third table companion. One doesn't hear much from him. Young Mr. Van Daan is very quiet and doesn't draw much attention to himself. As for appetite: a Danaïdean vessel, which is never full and after the heartiest meal declares quite calmly that he could have eaten double.

Number four—Margot. Eats like a little mouse and doesn't talk at all. The only things that go down are vegetables and fruit. "Spoiled" is the Van Daans' judgment; "not enough fresh air and games" our opinion.

Beside her—Mummy. Good appetite, very

talkative. No one has the impression, as Mrs. Van Daan: this is the housewife. What is the difference? Well, Mrs. Van Daan does the cooking, and Mummy washes up and polishes.

Numbers six and seven. I won't say much about Daddy and me. The former is the most unassuming of all at table. He looks first to see if everyone else has something. He needs nothing himself, for the best things are for the children. He is the perfect example, and sitting beside him, the "Secret Annexes" "bundle of nerves."

Dr. Dussel. Helps himself, never looks up, eats and doesn't talk. And if one must talk, then for heaven's sake let it be about food. You don't quarrel about it, you only brag. Enormous helpings go down and the word "No" is never heard, never when the food is good, and not often when it's bad. Trousers wrapping his chest, red coat, black bedroom slippers, and horn-rimmed spectacles. That is how one sees him at the little table, always working, alternated only by his afternoon nap, food, and—his favorite spot—the lavatory. Three, four, five times a day someone stands impatiently in front of the door and wriggles, hopping from one foot to the other, hardly able to contain himself. Does it disturb him? Not a bit! From quarter past seven till half past, from half past twelve till one o'clock, from two till quarter past, from four till quarter past, from six till quarter past, and from half past eleven until twelve. One can make a note of it—these are the regular "sitting times." He won't come off or pay any heed to an imploring voice at the door, giving warning of approaching disaster!

Number nine isn't a member of the "Secret Annexe" family, but rather a companion in the house and at table. Elli has a healthy appetite. Leaves nothing on her plate and is not picky-and-choosy. She is easy to please and that is just what gives us pleasure. Cheerful and good-tempered, willing and good-natured, these are her characteristics.

Yours, Anne

Wednesday, 14 June, 1944

Dear Kitty,

My head is haunted by so many wishes and thoughts, accusations and reproaches. I'm really not as conceited as so many people seem to think, I know my own faults and shortcomings better than anyone, but the difference is that I also know that I want to improve, shall improve, and have already improved a great deal.

Why is it then, I so often ask myself, that everyone still thinks I'm so terribly knowing and forward? Am I so knowing? Is it that I really am, or that maybe the others aren't? That sounds queer, I realize now, but I shan't cross out the last sentence, because it really isn't so crazy. Everyone knows that Mrs. Van Daan, one of my chief accusers, is unintelligent. I might as well put it plainly and say "stupid." Stupid people usually can't take it if others do better than they do.

Mrs. Van Daan thinks I'm stupid because I'm not quite so lacking in intelligence as she is; she thinks I'm forward because she's even more so; she thinks my dresses are too short, because hers are even shorter. And that's also the reason that she thinks I'm knowing, because she's twice as bad about joining in over subjects she knows absolutely nothing about. But one of my favorite sayings is "There's no smoke without fire," and I readily admit that I'm knowing.

Now the trying part about me is that I criticize and scold myself far more than anyone else does. Then if Mummy adds her bit of advice the pile of sermons becomes so insurmountable that in my despair I become rude and start contradicting and then, of course, the old well-known Anne watchword comes back: "No one understands me!" This phrase sticks in my mind; I know it sounds silly, yet there is some truth in it. I often accuse myself to such an extent that I simply long for a word of comfort, for someone who could give me sound advice and also draw out some of my real self; but, alas, I keep on looking, but I haven't found anyone yet.

I know that you'll immediately think of Peter, won't you, Kit? It's like this: Peter loves me not as a lover but as a friend and grows more affectionate every day. But what is the mysterious something that holds us both back? I don't understand it myself. Sometimes I think that my terrible longing for him was exaggerated, yet that's really not it, because if I don't go up to see him for two days, then I long for him more desperately than ever before. Peter is good and he's a darling, but still there's no denying that there's a lot about him that disappoints me. Especially his dislike of religion and all his talk about food and various other things don't appeal to me. Yet I feel quite convinced that we shall never quarrel now that we've made that straightforward agreement together. Peter is a peace-loving person; he's tolerant and gives in very easily. He lets me say a lot of things to him that he would never accept from his mother, he tries most persistently to keep his things in order. And yet why should he keep his innermost self to himself and why am I never allowed there? By nature he is more closed-up than I am, I agree, but I know—

and from my own experience—that at some time or other even the most uncommunicative people long just as much, if not more, to find someone in whom they can confide.

Both Peter and I have spent our most meditative years in the "Secret Annexe." We often discuss the future, the past, and the present, but, as I've already said, I still seem to miss the real thing and yet I know that it's there.

Yours, Anne

Tuesday, 1 August, 1944

Dear Kitty,

"Little bundle of contradictions." That's how I ended my last letter and that's how I'm going to begin this one. "A little bundle of contradictions," can you tell me exactly what it is? What does contradiction mean? Like so many words, it can mean two things, contradiction from without and contradiction from within.

The first is the ordinary "not giving in easily, always knowing best, getting in the last word," *enfin,* all the unpleasant qualities for which I'm renowned. The second nobody knows about, that's my own secret.

I've already told you before that I have, as it were, a dual personality. One half embodies my exuberant cheerfulness, making fun of everything, my high-spiritedness, and above all, the way I take everything lightly. This includes not taking offense at a flirtation, a kiss, an embrace, a dirty joke. This side is usually lying in wait and pushes away the other, which is much better, deeper and purer. You must realize that no one knows Anne's better side and that's why most people find me so insufferable.

Certainly I'm a giddy clown for one afternoon, but then everyone's had enough of me for another month. Really, it's just the same as a love film is for deep-thinking people, simply a diversion, amusing just for once, something which is soon forgotten, not bad, but certainly not good. I loathe having to tell you this, but why shouldn't I, if I know it's true anyway? My lighter superficial side will always be too quick for the deeper side of me and that's why it will always win. You can't imagine how often I've already tried to push this Anne away, to cripple her, to hide her, because after all, she's only half of what's called Anne: but it doesn't work and I know, too, why it doesn't work.

I'm awfully scared that everyone who knows me as I always am will discover that I have another side, a finer and better side. I'm afraid they'll laugh at me, think I'm ridiculous and sentimental, not take me seriously. I'm used to not being taken seriously but it's only the "lighthearted" Anne that's used to it and can bear it, the "deeper" Anne is too frail for it. Sometimes, if I really compel the good Anne to take the stage for a quarter of an hour, she simply shrivels up as soon as she has to speak, and lets Anne number one take over, and before I realize it, she has disappeared.

Therefore, the nice Anne is never present in company, has not appeared one single time so far, but almost always predominates when we're alone. I know exactly how I'd like to be, how I am too . . . inside. But, alas, I'm only like that for myself. And perhaps that's why, no, I'm sure it's the reason why I say I've got a happy nature within and why other people think I've got a happy nature without. I am guided by the pure Anne within, but outside I'm nothing but a frolicsome little goat who's broken loose.

As I've already said, I never utter my real feelings about anything and that's how I've acquired the name of chaser-after-boys, flirt, know-all, reader of love stories. The cheerful Anne laughs about it, gives cheeky answers, shrugs her shoulders indifferently, behaves as if she doesn't care, but, oh dearie me, the quiet Anne's reactions are just the opposite. If I'm to be quite honest, then I must admit that it does hurt me, that I try terribly hard to change myself, but that I'm always fighting against a more powerful enemy. A voice sobs within me: "There you are, that's what's become of you: you're uncharitable, you look supercilious and peevish, people dislike you and all because you won't listen to the advice given you by your own better half." Oh, I would like to listen, but it doesn't work; if I'm quiet and serious, everyone thinks it's a new comedy and then I have to get out of it by turning it into a joke, not to mention my own family, who are sure to think I'm ill, make me swallow pills for headaches and nerves, feel my neck and my head to see whether I'm running a temperature, ask if I'm constipated and criticize me for being in a bad mood. I can't keep that up: if I'm watched to that extent, I start by getting snappy, then unhappy, and finally I twist my heart round again, so that the bad is on the outside and the good is on the inside and keep on trying to find a way of becoming what I would so like to be, and what I could be, if . . . there weren't any other people living in the world.

Yours, Anne

from Anne Frank Remembered

by Miep Gies with Alison Leslie Gold

The inhabitants of the Secret Annex could never have managed without the courageous help of their Dutch friends. In this passage, Miep tells how she was able to rescue Anne's diary, and how she found out the fate of her friends.

Outside Amsterdam, at Schiphol Airport, food parcels came raining down. Small tins of margarine, real butter, biscuits, sausages, bacon, chocolate, cheese, and egg powder. Airplanes flew over us quite low, and for the first time their drone caused no tightening at the throat. People ran up onto the rooftops and waved anything they could get their hands on—flags, bed sheets.

On Saturday morning, everybody seemed to be out on the streets as I went to my office. In spite of the news and the festivity, it was still quite dangerous. The Germans were beside themselves with anger. I heard that at the Dam Square, across from the old Hotel Krasnapolsky, the German soldiers had gone berserk and begun shooting into the crowd, killing quite a few people. But nothing stopped the celebrating. People continued to make fires and dance.

After work, I came home and said to Henk, "Come, Henk. Let's join the celebration." I pulled on his arm.

He shook his head. "No," he said. "I'll stay here. I don't feel like joining in the jubilation in the streets. Too much," he continued, "has happened in my country in these five years. Too many people have been taken away. Who knows how many will never return? Yes, I'm happy it's over, but I want to stay in and be quiet." I took down the blackout curtains. For the first night in five years, we could look outside and see the moon.

We heard that the German soldiers were assembling in various parts of Holland and then leaving. Suddenly, they were gone. More Allied planes came and dropped more food parcels. There was the feeling everywhere that a miracle had happened. We waited for the announcement that the dropped food would be distributed.

On the seventh of May we had a day off. Shouts rang out in the street that the Canadians were coming. I threw my apron down onto a chair and again ran out with everyone else from our neighborhood to wait for the liberators on Rijnstraat. People said they were coming "right away," but we waited and waited, and they did not come.

Finally, after three hours of waiting, we saw four small Canadian tanks cross the Amstel over the Berlage Bridge. After a short stop, they rode farther into town. The soldiers wore berets. Their uniforms were light brown short jackets and trousers which were pulled tight at the ankles.

The main force of the Canadian Army arrived on the eighth of May. This lasted the whole day. They came in many columns, but Henk and I had gone to our offices and couldn't watch the parade. We heard from our friends that the soldiers were very, very grubby. Nonetheless, the girls kissed them on their dirty faces. The Canadians waved, and gave out the first real cigarettes anyone had seen in years.

They marched into South Amsterdam, and continued on toward the Dam Square and the Royal Palace. Queen Wilhelmina had already returned to her beloved Holland, now devastated and almost starved. Our Queen was sixty-four years old now, the short, stout lady whom Churchill had called "the bravest man in England." Like our country, she had endured.

The celebrations continued for days. The Canadian and Dutch national anthems were played again and again. There were music and dancing in the streets; a barrel organ that had been found somewhere, old accordions played—anything that made music. Right away, people planted marigold seeds, so that the color that the Germans had forbidden, orange, the color of our Royal House, would grow.

People who had been in hiding came out onto the streets. Jews came out of hiding places, rubbing eyes that were unused to sunlight, their faces yellow and pinched and distrustful.

Church bells rang everywhere; streamers flew.

The liberators had brought us new Dutch bank notes which had been printed in England. All currency was wildly inflated, and there was nothing in the shops to buy.

To wake up and go through a whole day without any sense of danger was amazing. And right away, Henk and I and everyone else began waiting to see just who would be coming home to us.

Shocking, unimaginable accounts circulated of the liberation of the German concentration camps. Pictures were printed in the first free newspapers; eyewitness information, too. Through the occupation we'd heard rumors of gassings, murder, brutality, poor living conditions in these camps, but none of us could have imagined such atrocities. The facts had far surpassed even our most pessimistic imaginings. I couldn't read the stories and turned away from the photos. I couldn't allow myself to think about these reports. I needed to do everything I could to keep my optimism about our friends. It would have been unbearable to think otherwise.

Quickly, short-term repairs were begun—boards put across empty windows, bridges and tracks repaired in order that trains might run again. Everything was needed, but no one had anything.

Henk was assigned to the Centraal Station to greet returning people and provide them with referrals for help—help with money, ration cards, housing. He went every day and sat at a desk. People came back on military trucks, and then trains when some routes were returned to service.

Jews and others who had spent years as slaves of the Nazis had awaited their return to a liberated Holland. Now they began to come back, their faces shriveled so that it was impossible to tell their ages.

Jews from the camps all had blue numbers tattooed on their arms. Children who no longer knew their birthdays and names could not recognize their families because they had been separated for so long.

Some of those who straggled back to our River Quarter found other people living in their apartments. Others managed to get their apartment back because an NSBer had fled from it. Slowly, a small trickle of Jews began to return to our quarter. Lists of survivors of the concentration camps were posted daily.

I heard it said that where the Jews had looked like everyone else before, now, after what they had endured, those who returned looked different. But people hardly noticed because everyone had been through so much misery that no one had much interest in the suffering of others.

Every day Henk sat at his desk at the Centraal Station and processed people. To everyone he would ask, "Have you heard anything about Otto Frank?" or, "Have you seen Otto Frank and his wife, Edith Frank, or anything of their daughters, Margot Frank and Anne Frank?"

And always the head would shake, "No," and the next would shake, "No." Each, in turn, would know nothing of our friends.

A few days after the liberation, I was at work in the office when suddenly the electricity went back on. Click, just like that, we had electric light again.

Right away, we learned that Victor Kraler was alive, that in fact, he had escaped from the hands of the Germans and had been in hiding in his own home through the final days of the Hunger Winter, cared for by his wife. When he came back to the office, he told us about his escape:

"Most of the people in the Amersfoort camp where we were first sent were political prisoners of one sort or another, black marketeers, Christians who had hidden Jews. I was transferred from Amersfoort concentration camp to various forced labor camps, the last one quite close to the German border. One morning in winter, the camp was called to a roll call. Then a whole group of Dutchmen was marched out of the camp.

"I said to myself, I'll drop behind the group, and did, falling into step with some old German soldiers. These men were old and tired, and had had enough of the war. I thought, I'll talk to them in German and find out where we're all going. So I asked, and they said, 'We're going to walk to Germany. We're moving the whole camp to Germany.'

"I thought, Before I know it, I'll be in Hitler's Germany. I'll never be able to get out of there. So I began to drop behind again.

"Suddenly, out of nowhere, Spitfire planes appeared and started to dive down and strafe the area. The guards were yelling out, 'Lie down! Hit the dirt!' We were beside a cornfield. I jumped down into the field, and the attack went on, the fighters strafing the entire area.

"Finally, the planes flew away and the guards shouted, 'Up! March! Into position!' But I stayed where I was, hidden in the corn, holding my breath. And believe it or not, they marched off leaving me alone in the cornfield.

"I waited awhile, then crawled the opposite way in the corn. Finally, I felt safe and stood up and walked out of the field. I started to walk, and very soon came to a small country village. I began to get very nervous, as I was still wearing my prison uniform.

"At the edge of the village was a bicycle place. I thought, Better take a chance, and went inside. There was a Dutchman in the shop. I told him that I had just escaped from a prison camp. 'Can I have a bicycle?' I asked. 'I want to go home.'

"The man looked me over, then went to the back of the shop and pushed out an old but sturdy black bicycle. 'Here,' he said, pushing it toward me, 'go home. After the war you can return the bicycle.'

"I pedaled home, and my wife hid me through the Hunger Winter until now."

Within a few weeks, goods began to appear in shopwindows—a winter coat, a pretty dress; but only in the windows. Nothing was for sale in the shops. A sign in the window of the shop would say FOR DISPLAY ONLY. Other shops showed cardboard imitations of milk bottles, cheese, and packets of good Dutch butter.

I heard that groups of Dutch children were being organized by the Allies for health holidays in Britain. These children were in such states of distress that something extraordinary was needed to build them up quickly.

Just as I had been sent from Vienna to Holland in 1920 as a hungry child with a tag around my neck, these Dutch children were put on ships in 1945 and sent across the North Sea to England for nourishment.

Day after day, Henk went to the Centraal Station and gave vouchers to returning Dutchmen, most of whom had lost everything and had either lost or been separated from their families. Day after day, he would ask, "Do you know Otto Frank? Have you seen the Frank family—Otto, Edith, Margot, and Anne?" And day after day, head after head would shake, "No." Or, "No, I have not seen or heard of these people."

Undaunted by this, Henk would ask the next person, and the next, "Do you know the Franks?" Always expecting one more ravaged head to shake, he finally heard a voice reply to his question, "Mister, I have seen Otto Frank, and he is coming back!"

Henk flew home that day to tell me. It was June 3, 1945. He ran into the living room and grabbed me. "Miep, Otto Frank is coming back!"

My heart took flight. Deep down I'd always known that he would, that the others would, too.

Just then, my eye caught sight of a figure passing outside our window. My throat closed. I ran outside.

There was Mr. Frank himself, walking toward our door.

We looked at each other. There were no words. He was thin, but he'd always been thin. He carried a little bundle. My eyes swam. My heart melted. Suddenly, I was afraid to know more. I didn't want to know what had happened. I knew I would not ask.

We stood facing each other, speechless. Finally, Frank spoke.

"Miep," he said quietly. "Miep, Edith is not coming back."

My throat was pierced. I tried to hide my reaction to his thunderbolt. "Come inside," I insisted.

He went on. "But I have great hope for Margot and Anne."

"Yes. Great hope," I echoed encouragingly. "Come inside."

He still stood there. "Miep, I came here because you and Henk are the ones closest to me who are still here."

I grabbed his bundle from his hand. "Come, you stay right here with us. Now, some food. You have a room here with us for as long as you want."

He came inside. I made up a bedroom for him, and put everything we had into a fine meal for him. We ate. Mr. Frank told us he had ended up in Auschwitz. That was the last time he'd seen Edith, Margot, and Anne. The men had been separated from the women immediately. When the Russians liberated the camp in January, he had been taken on a very long trip to Odessa. Then from there to Marseille by ship, and at last, by train and truck to Holland.

He told us these few things in his soft voice. He spoke very little, but between us there was no need for words.

Mr. Frank settled in with Henk and me. Right away, he came back to the office and took his place again as the head of the business. I know he was relieved to have something to do each day. Meanwhile, he began exploring the network of information on Jews in the camps—the refugee agencies, the daily lists, the most crucial word-of-mouth information—trying everything to get news about Margot and Anne.

When Auschwitz was liberated, Otto Frank had gone right away to the women's camp to find out about his wife and children. In the chaos and desolation of the camps, he had learned that Edith had died shortly before the liberation.

He had also learned that in all likelihood, Margot and Anne had been transferred to another camp, along with Mrs. van Daan. The camp was called Bergen-Belsen, and was quite a distance from Auschwitz. That was as far as his trail had gone so far, though. Now he was trying to pick up the search.

As to the other men, Mr. Frank had lost track of Albert Dussel. He had no idea what had happened to him after the transit camp of Westerbork. He had seen with his own eyes Mr. van Daan on his way to be gassed. And Peter van Daan had come to visit Frank in the Auschwitz infirmary. Mr. Frank knew that right before the liberation of the camp, the Germans had taken groups of prisoners with them in their retreat. Peter had been in one of these groups.

Otto Frank had begged Peter to try to get into the infirmary himself, but Peter couldn't or wouldn't. He had last been seen going off with the retreating Germans into the snow-covered countryside. There was no further news about him.

Mr. Frank held high hopes for the girls, because Bergen-Belsen was not a death camp. There were no gassings there. It was a work camp—filled with hunger and disease, but with no apparatus for liquidation. Because Margot and Anne had been sent to the camp later than most other inmates they were relatively healthy. I too lived on hope for Margot and Anne. In some deep part of me, like a rock, I counted on their survival and their safe return to Amsterdam.

Mr. Frank had written for news to several Dutch people who he had learned had been in Bergen-Belsen. Through word of mouth people were being reunited every day. Daily, he waited for answers to his letters and for the new lists of survivors to be released and posted. Every time there was a knock at the door or footfalls on the steps, all our hearts would stand still. Perhaps Margot and Anne had found their way back home, and we could see them with our own eyes at last. Anne's sixteenth birthday was coming on June 12. Perhaps, we hoped, . . . but then the birthday came and went, and still no news.

Mrs. Samson returned to Hunzestraat. She moved back into her room. Her granddaughter had died of diphtheria in hiding in Utrecht, but her little grandson was alive. So far, Mrs. Samson had had no news of her daughter and son-in-law, who had disappeared that day at the Centraal Station. Nothing had yet been heard from her husband, reputed to be in England. She too was in a limbo of waiting for news.

Our vegetable man came back from the camp with frozen feet. I saw him back in his shop, and we greeted each other like long-lost friends.

Still, the shops were almost empty; we lived on rations. But reconstruction and renewal were in the works. Our spice company sold mostly *ersatz* goods, but business trickled in, keeping the company going.

One morning, Mr. Frank and I were alone in the office, opening mail. He was standing beside me, and I was sitting at my desk. I was vaguely aware of the sound of a letter being slit open. Then, a moment of silence. Something made me look away from my mail. Then, Otto Frank's voice, toneless, totally crushed: "Miep."

My eyes looked up at him, seeking out his eyes.

"Miep." He gripped a sheet of paper in both his hands. "I've gotten a letter from the nurse in Rotterdam. Miep, Margot and Anne are not coming back."

We stayed there like that, both struck by lightning, burnt thoroughly through our hearts, our eyes fixed on each other's. Then Mr. Frank walked toward his office and said in that defeated voice, "I'll be in my office."

I heard him walk across the room and down the hall, and the door closed.

I sat at my desk utterly crushed. Everything that had happened before, I could somehow accept. Like it or not, I had to accept it. But this, I could not accept. It was the one thing I'd been sure would not happen.

I heard the others coming into the office. I heard a door opening and a voice chattering. Then, good-morning greetings and coffee cups. I reached into the drawer on the side of my desk and took out the papers that had been waiting there for Anne for nearly a year now. No one, including me, had touched them. Now Anne was not coming back for her diary.

I took out all the papers, placing the little red-orange checkered diary on top, and carried everything into Mr. Frank's office.

Frank was sitting at his desk, his eyes murky with shock. I held out the diary and the papers to him. I said, "Here is your daughter Anne's legacy to you."

I could tell that he recognized the diary. He had given it to her just over three years before, on her thirteenth birthday, right before going into hiding. He touched it with the tips of his fingers. I pressed everything into his hands; then I left his office, closing the door quietly.

Shortly afterward, the phone on my desk rang. It was Mr. Frank's voice. "Miep, please see to it that I'm not disturbed," he said.

"I've already done that," I replied.

Anne, so small then, coming out with pretty Margot to greet the adults and have a piece of cake. Anne would hold her cat, Moortje, in her arms, and she would dangle down nearly to the floor, almost too heavy for a small girl to hold.

Quickly, I put these thoughts aside. I wanted not to think about what had been before.

One day, two bicycles arrived for Mr. Frank from friends of his in England. "Miep," Frank told me, pushing a sleek, shiny new English bicycle toward me. "One for you and one for me." I took it. I had never before in my life had a brand-new bicycle. No one in the neighborhood had anything new. I imagine that they eyed our new bicycles jealously.

Another package arrived for Mr. Frank. This one bore elaborate labels from America, from friends who had safely spent the war there. Otto opened the package carefully. We both looked at the contents spread across the table.

There were tins, and American cigarettes, and several small packets. Frank suggested I open them and take a look at what there was. The first I opened sent an aroma of cocoa up into my face. It was overwhelming. I felt the texture, so soft and powdery, the color so dark brown.

Seeing it and smelling the cocoa, I began to cry.

Otto said, "Take it, make it."

I couldn't stop crying. It was unbelievable to me that I was seeing real cocoa again.

The final lists of Jewish survivors were posted by the Red Cross. Of those who had been deported by the Germans, very few had returned to the Netherlands—not even one in twenty. Of those who had gone into hiding, at least one-third had survived. All those who had survived had lost just about everything.

Mr. Frank's lodger, the man Henk and I had played our charade with, had been deported to the camps. But he had survived and come back. The older man who had asked us to keep his beautiful Shakespeare had not come back. So the book remained on our shelves, just in case he ever returned. Neither had my upstairs neighbor come back, the lady who had asked us to care for her cat, Berry. So Berry lived on with us.

Slowly, bit by bit, we learned that Albert Dussel had died in the Neuengamme camp. That Petronella van Daan had died either in Buchenwald or in Theresienstadt on the day it was liberated. That Peter van Daan hadn't died on the death march away from Auschwitz, but had somehow survived it and been placed in Mauthausen, only to die there on the very day that the camp was liberated by the Americans.

Through information gathered from eyewitness survivors, we learned that Margot and Anne had been separated at Auschwitz from their mother, Edith Frank, who had spent the last weeks of her life there alone. Margot and Anne had been transferred to Bergen-Belsen, where they had been relatively healthy at first, but then, in the early months of 1945, had both fallen ill with typhus. In February or March, Margot had succumbed, and then Anne, totally alone, had succumbed to typhus as well, just a few short weeks before the liberation of the camp.

Even though the final lists of survivors had been

posted, there were many displaced persons, and borders were not what they had been, so there was no way to know for sure the fate of many others who did not return. For some, it was possible to not give up hope.

Never once did we hear from Karel van der Hart after the war, but we heard somewhere that he'd gone to America.

In the evenings, after Henk, Otto, and I had returned from our offices and I'd fixed our evening meal, Otto began to translate bits of Anne's diary into German for his mother, who lived in Basel. Mr. Frank would include these translations with his letters to her. Sometimes he'd come walking out of his room holding Anne's little diary and shaking his head. He'd say to me, "Miep, you should hear this description that Anne wrote here! Who'd have imagined how vivid her imagination was all the while?"

But when he would ask me to listen to what she'd written, I'd have to say no. I could not bring myself to listen. It was much too upsetting to me.

Because of Frits van Matto's unsympathetic personality, Jo Koophuis and Otto Frank gently nudged him out of the business. They didn't fire him, but they persuaded him that he might have more of a future elsewhere. New warehousemen were hired.

Nineteen forty-six came and still we stayed poor; still there was nothing.

On the fifteenth of May, 1946, Elli Vossen got married and left the Prinsengracht. A young man was hired to take Elli's place. Coming as she did from a big family, six sisters and one brother, Elli had always dreamed of having a big family of her own. Right away, she was pregnant, and very happy that her lifelong dream was so quickly starting to come true.

I was now past my middle thirties. My childbearing years were quickly passing. My own dream of motherhood had greatly changed because of what had happened in Holland. I was glad no child of ours had had to endure the terrible war years. After the war we did not bring up the subject of having children.

I also had a great deal of trouble believing anymore in the existence of God. When I'd been a little girl in Vienna, my parents had been practicing Catholics. They took me to church a few times, but I didn't like it. I was such a little girl—maybe three, four, or five—I didn't really understand what was going on in the service, but I felt affected by the darkness of the huge church, and by its enormous size and the cold I felt inside. My aversion to church made me beg to be excused from attending. My parents didn't insist that I go. So I never went back.

When I came to Leiden, my adoptive family never made me go to church either, so as I grew up, I didn't conform to any religion. Always, though, I never doubted the existence of God. That is, until the war. Then, by the time the war was finished, my sense of God had been poisoned and only an empty hole was left.

Henk had been a nonbeliever before and throughout the war, and he continued that way.

But I had a craving to read on the subject, and I began to read the Old Testament. Then I read the New Testament. Then, with deep interest, I read studies of many different religions: books on Judaism, books on Catholicism, Protestantism, anything I could lay my hands on.

I never spoke about my reading to anyone. I just read and read. Everything I read was rich and interesting, yet I was always hungry for more. The dark years had pulled down my inner supports, and I was looking for something to replace them.

Although a slow reconstruction and renewal was taking place, we Dutch continued to harbor a deep and strong feeling of hatred for the suffering we'd been made to endure at the hands of our savage German oppressors. For five solid years we'd been without contact with the outside world. We'd been utterly humiliated, brought to our knees; the lives of good, innocent people had been interrupted and destroyed. We felt no stirrings of forgiveness.

In 1946, Queen Wilhelmina called our first national elections. Anton Mussert, the head of the Dutch NSB, was executed by a firing squad in The Hague, and Arthur Seyss-Inquart, the Nazi Reichskommissar of the Netherlands, was hanged after a trial at Nürnberg. People argued back and forth about what was "right" in wartime and what was "wrong." Many traitors were punished. But somehow, revenge and justice brought little satisfaction.

In December of 1946, we decided to move into another apartment in our quarter. We'd stayed much too long with Henk's sister on Hunzestraat. Henk and I had a friend whose wife had recently died, a Mr. van Caspel. He had a large apartment to himself and a small daughter, a girl of nine, away in boarding school. He invited us to share his rooms.

Henk and I discussed the situation with Otto. Otto said that if it was all right, he'd like to move along with us to this apartment. Naturally, we said he'd be very welcome to stay with us, but we knew that he had so many friends and contacts that he could probably find better lodgings than what we had found.

"I prefer staying with you, Miep," he explained. "That way I can talk to you about my family if I want."

In fact, Mr. Frank rarely talked about them, but I

understood what he meant. He could talk about his family if he wanted to. And if he didn't want to, in silence we all shared the same sorrow and memories.

So Otto, Henk, and I moved to Jekerstraat 65 together as 1947 began. Henk had begun to have a headache every day, a blinding headache. Not one to complain about himself, he said little about these headaches and did his best to go on about his daily business.

Every Saturday night, Henk and I, Mrs. Dussel, and several other friends would gather and play canasta together. Mr. Frank never played with us. But he had begun to have small gatherings of friends for coffee on Sundays. These were all Jews who had survived untold suffering. They'd come together on Sunday afternoons, asking one another, "Who's left in your family?" or "Did your wife come back?" or "What about your children? Your parents?" They'd exchange information about where they'd been— Auschwitz, Sobibor—facts about transports, dates; but never about what had happened to them personally. I could see that it was too difficult to talk about many things, and when they were together, it was not necessary.

At one of these Sunday get-togethers Frank mentioned that he had a diary written by his daughter Anne. One of the men at the gathering asked Frank if he might read it. Mr. Frank was reluctant, but gave the man some of the bits that he had translated for his mother in Basel, the sections that he'd been unsuccessfully trying for more than a year to get me to read.

After he'd read the excerpts, this man asked Frank if he might read the whole diary, that he was very much impressed with the excerpts and had a great curiosity to read more. Again with great reluctance, Mr. Frank gave him more to read.

Then the man asked Frank for permission to show the diary to a friend of his, a well-known historian. Frank was against it, but his friend cajoled and cajoled, and finally Frank said yes.

After he had read Anne's diary, the historian wrote an article about it for the Dutch newspaper *Het Parool,* which was now thriving, but had started as an underground paper during the war. The historian began a campaign to get Mr. Frank to allow Anne's diary to be published. Frank was very much against such a thing, and was adamant in his refusal. The historian and his friend eventually persuaded Otto Frank. They said that it was Frank's duty to share Anne's story with others, that her diary was a war document and very important because it expressed a unique voice of a young person in hiding.

So much persuasion began to make Frank feel that it was his duty to forgo his own sense of invaded privacy. Finally, although very reluctant, Frank agreed to allow a small, edited edition to be printed by Contact Publishers in Amsterdam. It was printed with the title *Het Achterhuis* (*"The Annex"*). Again and again, after it was published, Otto would ask me to read Anne's writing, but I continued to refuse. I simply could not bring myself to do it.

The printing of *Het Achterhuis,* which was Anne's name for the hiding place, was praised in some quarters, but there was indifference on the part of many people who had lived through such unpleasant situations themselves. The last thing they wanted was to read about such experiences. No one in Holland had had an easy time during the war. Most people had suffered immeasurably. Most people wanted to forget the war, to put it behind them and move on.

Nonetheless, Anne's diary was reprinted and gathered a wider audience. Always Otto would tell me, "Miep, you must read it." But always I couldn't. I couldn't relive the miseries, and I wouldn't rekindle the terrible losses.

Henk too declined to read Anne's words.

At last, food supplies, though still sparse, were being restored. Again healthy, fat Dutch cows grazed in the countryside. The trains began to run again, and the Amsterdam streetcars as well. Rubble had been cleared away.

During the occupation, there had been just two kinds of Dutch people: those who collaborated and those who resisted. Political and religious and class differences had been forgotten. It was simply we Dutch against our German oppressor.

After the liberation, the unity quickly disappeared and people again divided into groups and factions that were at odds with each other. Everyone returned to his old ways, to his own class, to his own political group. People had changed less than I would have thought.

Many who had moved into the Jewish apartments in South Amsterdam had stayed on. The neighborhood no longer had a Jewish flavor. In fact, there was not much in common among people in the neighborhood anymore. It had lost its distinctive progressive atmosphere. It would never be the same as before. Amsterdam was changed too, a modern city rather than the friendly town it had been.

With three grown men now at home—Henk, Otto, and Mr. van Caspel—there was much I needed to do to care for them properly. Sometimes van Caspel's daughter would come to spend a weekend with us. It was important to me that our home be clean and tidy and meals always be served on time. Mending needed to be done, and washing. And everyone needed a ready ear for listening.

At the office, real products were again for sale. The business had never ceased to function at any time. Since his return, Otto Frank had become once more the slightly nervous, soft-spoken man he'd been before the hiding time. The change that had taken place when he'd gone into hiding, the calm, authoritative personality he'd assumed, had vanished.

But Frank's interest in the business seemed to be waning. Since the publication of Anne's diary, letters had begun to come to him from children and adults. Conscientiously, Mr. Frank answered each letter. His office on the Prinsengracht became the place where he conducted matters pertaining to Anne's diary.

Then on a beautiful, warm day in 1947, I rode my bicycle to the Prinsengracht for the last time. Quietly, I said goodbye to everyone. I had given notice that I would no longer be employed by the firm. I was now fully responsible for the care of three men. I had decided that the care of these men and our home was now my full-time job. I was no longer the young girl longing for the freedom and independence that a job would give. Nothing in Amsterdam was as it had been before, and neither was I.

The second printing of the diary sold out and another printing was planned. Mr. Frank was approached with the idea of permitting the diary to be translated and published abroad. He was against it at first, but then he succumbed to the pressure on him to allow the diary a more widespread audience.

Again and again, he'd say to me, "Miep, you must read Anne's writing. Who would have imagined what went on in her quick little mind?" Otto was never discouraged by my continuing refusal. He would always wait awhile and then ask me again.

Finally, I gave in to his insistence. I said, "All right, I will read the diary, but only when I'm totally alone."

The next time I was totally alone, on a warm day, I took the second printing of the diary, went to my room, and shut the door.

With awful fear in my heart, I opened the book and turned to the first page.

And so I began to read.

I read the whole diary without stopping. From the first word, I heard Anne's voice come back to speak to me from where she had gone. I lost track of time. Anne's voice tumbled out of the book, so full of life, moods, curiosity, feelings. She was no longer gone and destroyed. She was alive again in my mind.

I read to the very end. I was surprised by how much had happened in hiding that I'd known nothing about. Immediately, I was thankful that I hadn't read the diary after the arrest, during the final nine months of the occupation, while it had stayed in my desk drawer right beside me every day. Had I read it, I would have had to burn the diary because it would have been too dangerous for people about whom Anne had written.

When I had read the last word, I didn't feel the pain I'd anticipated. I was glad I'd read it at last. The emptiness in my heart was eased. So much had been lost, but now Anne's voice would never be lost. My young friend had left a remarkable legacy to the world.

But always, every day of my life, I've wished that things had been different. That even had Anne's diary been lost to the world, Anne and the others might somehow have been saved.

Not a day goes by that I do not grieve for them.

Elegy for Anne Frank

by Jessica Smith

This poem is one of many testimonies of how Anne Frank's diary continues to touch us more than 50 years after her death.

You blossomed and grew
between the quiet gray walls
of your attic home.
A sidewalk-surrounded flower
5   pushed up through the cracks,
petals straining for
the light, but your
roots held you down.

In the dim light of your room
10   you made family trees,
the continuing lives
comforting you in ways
your mother could not.

While concentration camps
15   built bonfires with the
bones of your neighbors,
you dreamed of the sun and
the love you'd find when the doors
of your prison were unlocked.

20   When I took your short life from your diary,
I could feel your heartbeat

pulse with my own,
and every breath you took
went into my own lungs,
25 every desire you felt,
I felt, too.

Your life was held by four silent years,
surrounding you as the four walls did.
And before the last bomb fell,
30 destroying the last of your love and light,
you died.

I am thankful.

Bubili: A Young Gypsy's Fight for Survival

by Ina R. Friedman

Unfortunately Hitler's hatred spread to many nationalities and ethnic groups. This selection shows how one boy used his wits and every resource he could muster to survive the Nazi persecution of Gypsies in Hungary.

Persons under protective arrest, Jews, Gypsies, and
Russians . . . would be delivered by the Ministry of
Justice to the S. S. to be worked to death.
—Order issued by Heinrich Himmler, September 18, 1942

Even though they are the descendants of ancient tribes from Northern India, the Romani were called Gypsies by Europeans. The Europeans thought they had migrated from Egypt because of their dark skin and did not seem to realize that the Romani were composed of several tribes, the largest being the Sinti and Roma. Grouped into one category, "Gypsies," they were persecuted throughout the centuries. In this, the Germans were no exception.

Of all Hitler's intended victims, only Gypsies and

Jews were to be exterminated completely. No member of these groups, from infants to grandparents, was to be permitted to live. To justify their complete destruction, the Nazis labeled them socially "inferior," "racially impure," and "criminals." German scientists were ordered to conduct sham medical experiments to prove the Gypsies' inadequacy by measuring their skulls. Other medical experiments were created to demonstrate falsely that Romani blood was different from so-called normal blood. These absurd claims were hailed by the Germans who wanted to believe in their own superiority.

The Romani, like the Jews, were natural scapegoats. Both groups were outsiders, the Jews because they were not Christians, the Romani for various reasons. When the dark-skinned Romani first arrived in Eastern Europe in the early 1300s (after centuries of migration from their native India), they appeared strange to the Europeans. They spoke a language unlike any other ever heard in Europe. Since they could not claim land that was already occupied, they lived in wagons. Because they had come via Turkey, Europeans thought they were Muslims. They were not. Neither were they Christians. When they adopted Christianity to conform to the country in which they lived, they still held on to their Romani customs. They had their own rules and taboos.

At that time, European craftsmen belonged to guilds or unions. These guilds decided who would be employed. Outsiders, such as Jews and Romani, were not allowed to join the guilds. Since they could read and write, the Jews sought other occupations. But the Romani, who were illiterate, had only their ancient trades as armor makers, basket weavers, musicians, jewelers, and horse traders with which to earn a living. The superiority of their work made them a threat to local craftsmen. Because they were kept out of the marketplace, many Romani had to live by their wits.

Even when they attempted to join the church, they were not welcome. Their fortunetelling and "ability to predict the future" made the priests fear them. In the Middle Ages, the uneducated peasants were very superstitious. The church wanted the people to believe only what the priests told them. The church did not want the Romani giving people other forms of hope or fear.

While they were feared by competitors and despised as a people, the Romani were prized for their skills. In the Balkan countries, they were enslaved in the fourteenth century by monasteries and landowners and it was not until the nineteenth century that slavery was abolished in eastern Europe.

To escape oppression, many Romani fled to western and northern Europe in the fifteenth century. However, as soon as they arrived, the various countries passed laws to keep them out. Rewards were offered for Gypsies, dead or alive. In some places, if a Gypsy woman was discovered, her left ear was cut off. Gypsy hunting was an accepted pastime. In nineteenth-century Denmark, one hunt "bagged" 260 men, women, and children.

Hatreds do not easily disappear. The foundations for the Nazis' policies against the Romani were laid in 1899, long before Hitler came to power. A "Central Office for the Fighting of the Gypsy Menace" was established in Munich. By 1920, all Romani were forced to be photographed and fingerprinted because of their so-called criminal tendencies.

The Nazis' first proposal to rid Germany of the "Gypsy Menace" was suggested in 1933. Thirty thousand Romani were to be sent out to sea and the ships sunk. Fortunately, this plan was abandoned. However, many Romani were sterilized at that time. The sterilizations were carried out under a newly passed law permitting the sterilization of "mentally defectives."

In 1935, under the Nuremberg Laws, Jews and Gypsies were declared second-class citizens. Any individual who had two Romani great-grandparents out of eight great-grandparents was declared a Gypsy. Many of these people had been assimilated into the German population and were unaware of their Romani heritage.

In 1936, four hundred Bavarian Romani were sent to the Dachau concentration camp. Mass roundups of Sinti began in 1938. Some of those rounded up had sons in the German army. By March 1939, the law required all Romani to register at the "Central Office for the Fight Against the Gypsy Menace." The invasion of Poland brought orders to the *Einsatzgruppen* (the Nazi extermination units) to round up and murder all Gypsies, Jews, and Poles. Like the Jews, the Gypsies were moved into special areas and prevented from leaving. In 1940, a group of 250 Gypsy children from Brno, Czechoslovakia, were taken from their parents and used in an experiment to test the efficiency of Cyklon B, a poisonous gas.

All Sintis serving in the German army were removed from their units and sent to Auschwitz in 1942. Some arrived in uniform wearing the medals they had received for bravery. Most were gassed.

The Sinti and Romani who were not gassed were used in medical experiments. These included different methods of sterilization, without the use of anesthesia.

In Dachau, Romani were among the inmates used to determine how much salt water an individual could drink before dying. At Auschwitz, Dr. Josef Mengele used Gypsy twins for inhuman and scientifically unfounded experiments. He sent their organs to Kaiser Wilhelm Institute in Berlin for dissection.

At least half a million Romani were murdered by the Germans. As more and more Nazi records are discovered, the number grows. Countless others bear the scars of physical experiments and mental anguish caused by their own suffering in the camps and by the loss of their families.

Unfortunately, the persecution of the Romani continues. The West German government has never acknowledged the suffering of the Romani during the Holocaust. As of this writing, it has never paid reparations for the suffering of the Romani. Laws restricting the movements of the Romani are in effect in many lands. Even in the United States, some states still require Gypsies to be licensed.

The treatment of the Gypsies throughout the world is a continuing shame to all nations. Anton Fojn's story mirrors the treatment of the Romani by the Nazi government.

I cried when the prison barber clipped my hair and threw the locks into my lap. "A souvenir, Gypsy." At sixteen, I was very vain. My black wavy hair had reached to the nape of my neck. How could the Germans do this to me, Bubili, an Austrian Sinti? The barber put his hand on my shoulder to keep me from rising. "I'm not finished." With a dull razor, he shaved the rest of my head, my chest, my whole body. When he finished, my whole body ached. I stared at those standing next to me. My father, my uncles, and my cousins were unrecognizable, plucked birds from some strange planet.

And I? Without my hair, I was no longer Bubili. I was a piece of wood.

No, worse. Even a piece of wood could be used for something. We were trash, something to be thrown away. Why did the Germans have to strip us of our humanity?

The commandant and the S.S. men came into the room. They poked us as though we were cattle. "These Gypsy men are strong. Not like the Jews and the others who come here half starved. Why not send them to the army? Let them learn to fight for us."

"Orders are orders," the commandant said. "Treat them like the rest of the scum."

How did I arrive at Dachau concentration camp? I had never heard of the place.

When Hitler marched into Austria in March 1938, he first entered Linz and Vienna. I couldn't read. I wasn't aware of what the Nazis were doing in those cities. I lived in Klagenfurt, in southern Austria. For a few days, nothing happened.

One night, I went to the movies. Before I entered the theater at seven o'clock, I heard people shouting "Heil Schuschnigg." Schuschnigg was prime minister of Austria before the invasion. At nine o'clock, when I came out, people were yelling "Heil Hitler."

I stopped a man on the street. "What kind of a cattle call is 'Heil Hitler'?"

"Be quiet," the man whispered. "The Germans have just entered Klagenfurt. You'd better go home as fast as you can. Stick to the side streets. Don't let them see you."

My father was relieved when I walked into our house. "Bubili, I don't want you going into the center of town. We have to learn what the Germans have in mind for our people," he said. My father could read. He knew about Hitler's threats.

I was fifteen. I couldn't understand what was going on. When one of my uncles was taken to the hospital, I set out to bring him some food. As I walked toward the *Lindwurmplatz*, I noticed men in long leather coats talking to the police. I didn't know a Gestapo from a giraffe. An Austrian policeman grabbed me by the arm. "Hey, dark one, where are your papers?"

"My father has them. Come with me to my house."

Instead, he threw me in jail.

"Why are you locking me up? I haven't done anything."

"The Germans are the authority here. I don't know why they want you. Perhaps they'll send you to Germany, to a concentration camp." The policeman slammed and locked the cell door.

I looked at the other prisoner. "Tell me, please, what does 'concentration camp' mean? The policeman thinks the Germans want to send me there."

The prisoner looked frightened. He shrank into the corner, as though I was poison. "It's a death camp."

"Death camp? I have to escape." I looked around. The only opening was a narrow window with bars. It overlooked the exercise yard.

"It's impossible," the other man said. "No one can escape from this cell. You're a dead man."

"No, I am Bubili."

The cell door opened, and the guard shoved in a

drunk. "I know, I know, there are only two cots, but he'll be gone by tomorrow."

The drunk collapsed on the floor and started to snore. I searched his pocket for cigarettes and found a knife. As he slept, I moved the knife back and forth across the radiator to make sharp teeth like a saw.

In the morning, the guard removed the drunk. I poked around the mortar surrounding the window. "There's wood here," I whispered to my cellmate. "Lie down with your ear to the floor. Whistle if you hear the guard coming."

The guards went around in felt slippers. You could only hear them if you kept your ear to the floor.

I worked like crazy, moving the knife back and forth until I made a hole alongside the window. I sawed until it was big enough for my head to go through. I was slim and wiry. Late that night, the other prisoner followed me through the hole onto the tin roof. It was raining, and the sound of the rain on the roof dulled all other noises. I hung from the roof by my hands and dropped to the ground. The other man followed. I led him through the back alleys to the woods. For several days we walked until we came to the Yugoslavian border. My father and I had crossed over into Yugoslavia many times with our racehorses. Father was also a violinist. He played in taverns in towns on both sides of the border so I was familiar with the area. When we came to the outskirts of Slovenia, I cautioned my companion, "If we bump into a policeman, act natural. For God's sake, don't panic and run."

A few blocks from the border, we saw a policeman patrolling the street. Right away, the other guy took off. Before I knew it, we were behind bars again. How could I get out of this prison? When the guard opened the door the next day, he said, "Go back where you belong, Gypsy," and led us to the Austrian border.

I was afraid to go home. Instead of returning to Austria, I made my way toward another section of the Yugoslavian border. I was used to surviving in the woods. I caught rabbits and squirrels and roasted them over a fire. For months I lived on the run in Yugoslavia, in and out of prison. Eventually I decided Yugoslavia was too hot for me, and I went to Hungary. There, I met a Sinti who had lost his wife. I took care of his two young children while he worked. In the evenings, I went to taverns where there were Sinti musicians and danced to earn money. I had studied ballet and was a good dancer. One night the police burst into the tavern. The musicians stopped in the middle of their song.

"Line up, Gypsies," The policeman shouted.

The musicians stood there with their instruments. Romani who had come to hear them were arrested, too. We were marched toward the railroad station. As we stood there waiting for a train, I darted into a crowd of people. The police were afraid to shoot. I jumped into the Danube River and swam until it was safe to go ashore.

Dripping wet, I entered a tavern across the border in Bratislava, Czechoslovakia. "Where God wills," as we say, "one meets Gypsies." After the tavern closed, I walked down the street and met four Gypsy musicians returning home from an evening's work.

"Ah, Bubili, we know your father," the violinist said. "Stay with us until we can find news of your family."

Months passed, but none of the Romani who traveled past the campsite had heard anything.

"I'm going back," I told my friends. "I have to know what is happening to my family."

"It might not be safe," my father's friend said. "It's unusual for our network not to have any news. Stay with us."

It was 1939. I had been away from home for more than a year. I "borrowed" a bicycle and arrived in Graz, Austria, around midnight. At the *Gasthaus Hasenwirt,* I went to the owner. We had always stopped at this inn to take care of the horses. "Where is my family?"

"Bubili, I don't know. The Germans have locked up many Sinti. But I think there are still some at Bruck an der Mur. Your father may be among them."

Bruck an der Mur was in the Austrian Alps, a good thirty-five miles away. I left immediately, using the darkness to make my way through the streets into the forest. I dared not be seen. A day later, I reached our circle of wagons high in the mountains. My uncle was astonished to see me. "Bubili, we thought you were dead."

My father, my grandmother, my uncles, and my aunts crowded around to hug me.

After my grandmother had fed me some stew from the kettle, I lay down to rest. "Tomorrow," my father said, "go to your mother's brother in Leoben. I think you will be safer there." My mother had died two years earlier.

The next morning, I hiked through the mountains to Leoben, beside the river. My mother's family welcomed me. That night, my uncle and I went to a tavern. As the tavern owner shook my uncle's hand to welcome him, he whispered, "Blauch, take off. A drunken policeman boasted of a Gypsy roundup tomorrow. You'll all be sent to a concentration camp."

"The Germans can't do anything to us. We are Austrian citizens," my uncle assured me, "but,

Bubili, let's get back to the wagons." The gaily painted wagons were grouped around the foot of a hill. At the top of the hill, there was a shed. Instead of sleeping on the ground next to my uncle's wagon, I took some quilts and went to sleep in the shed.

The next morning, June 26, 1939 (I can never forget the date), S.S. and Austrian police surrounded the wagons at daybreak. My aunt tried to signal me to leave. She sang as loudly as she could in our Romani language. "Bubili, run." But when one is young, one sleeps so well. When I did not wake up, she sang louder, "Run, run, the police are here. The Deathheads have come."

I grabbed my pants and started to jump out the door. A waiting S.S. man seized me. "You," he said, pushing me down the hill, "join the others."

"I'll help my uncle take the horses out of the stall so the horses can pull the wagon to the police station," I said.

"No," the S.S. man said. "Leave them in the stable. You'll pull the wagon yourself."

My uncle had only one leg. My aunt and I and two other Sintis harnessed ourselves to the wagon. Just outside the city, I tried to dart away. But the S.S. man grabbed me. The courtyard of the police station was already crowded with so many Sinti that we stood there like herrings crammed into a barrel.

While the police were registering the men, my aunt whispered, "Bubili, hide beneath my petticoat." Our women wore three and four skirts that touched the ground. I was very thin and agile and could easily have hidden.

"I can't. Uncle has only one foot. I have to help him."

The next day, the Germans forced all the men to climb into busses and trucks. I was the only young boy among 1,035 men. The women and children were released to go home. Where was my father?

My father had been picked up in an earlier raid on Bruck an der Mur. At the railroad station, he found out that my uncle and I had been taken. He asked the Germans to let us travel in the same boxcar. Two days later, June 28, the train stopped just outside the gates of Dachau. We waited, locked in the airless boxcar for about three quarters of an hour. Then we heard a shout as thirty or forty young S.S. men unlocked the bolts and threw open the doors. "Austrian pigheads," they screamed. "Out, out. Run, you Congo niggers, run." Their whips fell on us, killing two men as we ran toward the gates of Dachau.

"Line up. Faces to the sun." The whole square was filled with prisoners in striped uniforms. Many of them wore yellow stars on their shirts. The others had different colored triangles on their uniforms.

We stood on the assembly place, the sun beating down on us from early morning until three in the afternoon. If someone dropped, we were not allowed to pick him up. Then an S.S. man with a whip drove us into a building.

"Sit down," the guard said. He held a board with my name and number 34 016 across my chest. The photographer snapped my picture. With his foot, the photographer pushed a lever that punched a nail into my rear. Like a trained monkey, I jumped through the small window leading to the property room. Why couldn't they just tell us to get up instead of punching us with a nail?

In the property room, the guards shouted at us, "Take off all your clothes. Put everything else in the two baskets—your jewelry, your papers, your money." We stood there naked as the guards led us toward the showers. It was after the shower I lost my hair. I wondered what more could the Nazis do to us?

The prisoners in charge of the clothing laughed as they threw it at us. If you were tall, you got striped pants that were too short. If you were short, you got striped pants that were too long. I would not look any more ridiculous. I "found" thread and shortened my pants.

The shoes were even worse. Only the *kapos,* the prisoners in charge of other prisoners, and the block "elders" had leather shoes. The rest of us were thrown wooden clogs. The wooden shoes hurt and bruised my feet. I had to figure out how to get a pair of leather shoes. It was summer, and we were taken out to help the farmers bring in crops. At the risk of my life, I smuggled potatoes in my shirt into camp. The big commodity was *schnapps* (whiskey). By bartering, I got *schnapps,* which someone had stolen from the S.S. The *schnapps* I traded for leather shoes. We Romani have always been concerned about our hair, our teeth, and our shoes.

Inside Dachau, the prisoners were a mixed lot. The triangle on his uniform marked each man. Gypsies had brown triangles; political prisoners, red. The greens were the most feared. They were criminals who had been sent to Dachau. Often they were the block elders or worked in the administration. Jehovah's Witnesses wore purple triangles; homosexuals, pink. The Jews had two yellow triangles arranged into a Jewish star.

In September 1939, Germany invaded Poland and World War II began. Many of us were shipped to Buchenwald. Little did I know that I would consider Dachau heaven compared to Buchenwald. In Buchenwald, everything had to be done on the run.

"*Schnell, schnell* (faster, faster)," the guards shouted as we struggled to haul trees or dig trenches. Blows fell on our backs and necks. One of my uncles could not move quickly enough. An S.S. man bludgeoned him to death.

Every night, I fell asleep with a pain in my heart. I kept saying to myself, "I am Bubili. I will outlive those bastards. I will one day give testimony." I prayed for the luck that would help me to stay alive.

One morning, as we stood at roll call, shivering in the snow, the S.S. man shouted, "Everyone count out loud from one to seven. Every seventh man step forward." My father was lined up next to my mother's youngest brother. I was near the end of the line.

I began to sweat. Out of the corner of my eye, I tried to figure out whether my father and uncle were safe. I heard my father shout "Five." I breathed a sigh of relief. The counting grew closer. "Three," the man next to me called. "Thank God." I had survived the selections for death this time.

In December 1941 all Austrian Gypsies were shipped to Gusen 1, a labor camp in Austria. There, I was put in a separate barracks from my father and uncle. By luck, I had a good *kapo*. But I was concerned about my father. Though he was a powerful man, much taller than I, he had been weakened by lack of food. One day, when I returned from a work detail, I went looking for him. Five times I walked past him as he stood in front of his barracks, but I didn't recognize him. He had shrunken to half his size. I finally recognized him by his big nose. I was shocked when I realized his physical condition. I lifted him in my arms. He was as light as a child.

A week later, the *kapo* assigned me to work in

Gross-Rosen, another labor camp. When I saw the Germans were loading my father and one of my uncles onto a truck, I held back, saying, "I want to go with them."

"No, Bubili," the *kapo* snapped. "You go where I tell you."

When I came back that evening, I couldn't find my father. I ran into his barracks. He wasn't there. I ran through the grounds like a madman shouting, "Father, father, where are you?"

My block elder grabbed me. "It's too late, they were gassed on the truck. Calm down, otherwise you're finished."

For several days, I couldn't eat. The block elder talked to me. "If you don't eat, you'll be 'on the road to eternity.' Your father and uncle are gone. You have to do everything you can to stay alive."

Yes, I had to live to bear witness to this senseless machinery of human destruction. Again, I was lucky. The *kapo* helped me to get a job cooking for the S.S. They liked the stews that I had learned to make over the campfires. At last, I had enough to eat. I smuggled out food to the Sinti.

The days and years run together. In six years, I was in a total of ten camps. From hell to hell. In Mauthausen I was put in a punishment camp for fighting with another prisoner. Mauthausen was famous for its quarry with 180 steps, ironically called "the stairway to heaven." The prisoners had to carry stones up the steps. We were so weak, skeletons. The stones rubbed against our skin and left our legs raw. "Run, run, you Congo nigger," the guards shouted, flailing us with their whips. The steps were covered with the blood from wounded prisoners. Those who slipped fell to their death. I always tried to be in the center of the column so if I slipped, I wouldn't plunge over the side.

Toward the end of the war, I was sent to Gusen 2, another labor camp. I was surprised to find Jewish children in the camp. I thought they had all been killed, but here were sixteen children from eleven to sixteen years old. These children had been marked for death. Hitler wanted no one alive to bear witness.

I thought of my brother and my sisters, my nieces and my nephews, and wept. Somehow we had to save these few surviving children. Where they came from, where their parents were, nobody knew. By this time, there was no longer tight supervision in the camps. The younger, highly disciplined S.S. men had fled. Older, less murderous men now held command.

I went to my barracks elder, Juckel. "Juckel, how can we let the Germans murder these children? The war is almost over. They don't have to die."

"But their numbers have already been assigned for the transport to the crematorium. There's no way I can save them. Their numbers are down."

I shook my head. "No, Juckel, there are old people here who won't make it to next week. Trade their numbers for the children's numbers. You can hide the children until the Allies arrive. The new guards don't check like the others did."

He folded and refolded his blanket. "Where would we hide them? It's impossible."

"You're a good man, not like the others. It will be on your conscience," I said, turning toward the door. "Maybe you should talk it over with your friend, the camp elder, in the administration building. Records can be altered."

I went outside and began to play with the children.

Juckel left the barracks. A short while later he touched my arm, "Switch the numbers. If we're caught . . ."

Was I any better than the Nazis deciding who should live and who should die? These were older people, skeletons, barely able to walk. People without hope, *mussulmen* (zombies). Who had the greater right to live? The children or the *mussulmen*? I thought of my sisters and brother.

"Don't say anything," I told the children when I changed their numbers. "Just memorize your new number."

Juckel and the camp elder led the children away. Where they hid them, I don't know.

The fighting grew closer. More and more of the guards disappeared. When the Americans marched into the camp, I was hysterical with joy. I had survived. More than that, I had helped to save sixteen children.

Anton (Bubili) Fojn and his wife live in Hanau, Germany, where he is in the clothing business. They have four grown children. The sixteen children whom he helped to hide emigrated to Israel. Mr. Fojn is active in the Romani Union. Unlike the Jewish and deaf victims of the Nazis, the Romani have never received any compensation from the German government for their suffering during World War II. Mr. Fojn and the Romani Union are working to correct this inequity.

The Bracelet

by Yoshiko Uchida

*During World War II, many Japanese-
Americans in the West were forced to
leave behind their homes and businesses.
They were shipped off to internment
camps, where they lived out the war years
in barracks surrounded by guards and
fences. While these camps were far from
the Nazi death camps, they are a troubling
legacy. In this story, a young girl manages
to keep her hope and faith in others,
despite the injustices she suffers.*

"Mama, is it time to go?"

I hadn't planned to cry, but the tears came
suddenly, and I wiped them away with the back of
my hand. I didn't want my older sister to see me
crying.

"It's almost time, Ruri," my mother said gently.
Her face was filled with a kind of sadness I had never
seen before.

I looked around at my empty room. The clothes
that Mama always told me to hang up in the closet,
the junk piled on my dresser, the old rag doll I could
never bear to part with; they were all gone. There was
nothing left in my room, and there was nothing left in
the rest of the house. The rugs and furniture were
gone, the pictures and drapes were down, and the
closets and cupboards were empty. The house was
like a gift box after the nice thing inside was gone;
just a lot of nothingness.

It was almost time to leave our home, but we

weren't moving to a nicer house or to a new town. It was April 21, 1942. The United States and Japan were at war, and every Japanese person on the West Coast was being evacuated by the government to a concentration camp. Mama, my sister Keiko and I were being sent from our home, and out of Berkeley, and eventually, out of California.

The doorbell rang, and I ran to answer it before my sister could. I thought maybe by some miracle, a messenger from the government might be standing there, tall and proper and buttoned into a uniform, come to tell us it was all a terrible mistake; that we wouldn't have to leave after all. Or maybe the messenger would have a telegram from Papa, who was interned in a prisoner-of-war camp in Montana because he had worked for a Japanese business firm.

The FBI had come to pick up Papa and hundreds of other Japanese community leaders on the very day that Japanese planes had bombed Pearl Harbor. The government thought they were dangerous enemy aliens. If it weren't so sad, it would have been funny. Papa could no more be dangerous than the mayor of our city, and he was every bit as loyal to the United States. He had lived here since 1917.

When I opened the door, it wasn't a messenger from anywhere. It was my best friend, Laurie Madison, from next door. She was holding a package wrapped up like a birthday present, but she wasn't wearing her party dress, and her face drooped like a wilted tulip.

"Hi," she said. "I came to say good-bye."

She thrust the present at me and told me it was something to take to camp. "It's a bracelet," she said before I could open the package. "Put it on so you won't have to pack it." She knew I didn't have one inch of space left in my suitcase. We had been instructed to take only what we could carry into camp, and Mama had told us that we could each take only two suitcases.

"Then how are we ever going to pack the dishes and blankets and sheets they've told us to bring with us?" Keiko worried.

"I don't really know," Mama said, and she simply began packing those big impossible things into an enormous duffel bag—along with umbrellas, boots, a kettle, hot plate, and flashlight.

"Who's going to carry that huge sack?" I asked.

But Mama didn't worry about things like that. "Someone will help us," she said. "Don't worry." So I didn't.

Laurie wanted me to open her package and put on the bracelet before she left. It was a thin gold chain with a heart dangling on it. She helped me put it on, and I told her I'd never take it off, ever.

"Well, good-bye then," Laurie said awkwardly. "Come home soon."

"I will," I said, although I didn't know if I would ever get back to Berkeley again.

I watched Laurie go down the block, her long blond pigtails bouncing as she walked. I wondered who would be sitting in my desk at Lincoln Junior High now that I was gone. Laurie kept turning and waving, even walking backwards for a while, until she got to the corner. I didn't want to watch anymore, and I slammed the door shut.

The next time the doorbell rang, it was Mrs. Simpson, our other neighbor. She was going to drive us to the Congregational Church, which was the Civil Control Station where all the Japanese of Berkeley were supposed to report.

It was time to go. "Come on, Ruri. Get your things," my sister called to me.

It was a warm day, but I put on a sweater and my coat so I wouldn't have to carry them, and I picked up my two suitcases. Each one had a tag with my name and our family number on it. Every Japanese family had to register and get a number. We were Family Number 13453.

Mama was taking one last look around our house. She was going from room to room, as though she were trying to take a mental picture of the house she had lived in for fifteen years, so she would never forget it.

I saw her take a long last look at the garden that Papa loved. The irises beside the fish pond were just beginning to bloom. If Papa had been home, he would have cut the first iris blossom and brought it inside to Mama. "This one is for you," he would have said. And Mama would have smiled and said, "Thank you, Papa San," and put it in her favorite cut-glass vase.

But the garden looked shabby and forsaken now that Papa was gone and Mama was too busy to take care of it. It looked the way I felt, sort of empty and lonely and abandoned.

When Mrs. Simpson took us to the Civil Control Station, I felt even worse. I was scared, and for a minute I thought I was going to lose my breakfast right in front of everybody. There must have been over a thousand Japanese people gathered at the church. Some were old and some were young. Some were talking and laughing, and some were crying. I guess everybody else was scared too. No one knew exactly what was going to happen to us. We just knew we were being taken to the Tanforan Racetrack, which the army had turned into a camp for the Japanese. There were fourteen other camps like ours along the West Coast.

What scared me most were the soldiers standing at the doorway of the church hall. They were carrying guns with mounted bayonets. I wondered if they thought we would try to run away, and whether they'd shoot us or come after us with their bayonets if we did.

A long line of buses waited to take us to camp. There were trucks, too, for our baggage. And Mama was right; some men were there to help us load our duffel bag. When it was time to board the buses, I sat with Keiko and Mama sat behind us. The bus went down Grove Street and passed the small Japanese food store where Mama used to order her bean-curd cakes and pickled radish. The windows were all boarded up, but there was a sign still hanging on the door that read, "We are loyal Americans."

The crazy thing about the whole evacuation was that we were all loyal Americans. Most of us were citizens because we had been born here. But our parents, who had come from Japan, couldn't become citizens because there was a law that prevented any Asian from becoming a citizen. Now everybody with a Japanese face was being shipped off to concentration camps.

"It's stupid," Keiko muttered as we saw the racetrack looming up beside the highway. "If there were any Japanese spies around, they'd have gone back to Japan long ago."

"I'll say," I agreed. My sister was in high school and she ought to know, I thought.

When the bus turned into Tanforan, there were more armed guards at the gate, and I saw barbed wire strung around the entire grounds. I felt as though I were going into a prison, but I hadn't done anything wrong.

We streamed off the buses and poured into a huge

room, where doctors looked down our throats and peeled back our eyelids to see if we had any diseases. Then we were given our housing assignments. The man in charge gave Mama a slip of paper. We were in Barrack 16, Apartment 40.

"Mama!" I said. "We're going to live in an apartment!" The only apartment I had ever seen was the one my piano teacher lived in. It was in an enormous building in San Francisco with an elevator and thick carpeted hallways. I thought how wonderful it would be to have our own elevator. A house was all right, but an apartment seemed elegant and special.

We walked down the racetrack looking for Barrack 16. Mr. Noma, a friend of Papa's, helped us carry our bags. I was so busy looking around, I slipped and almost fell on the muddy track. Army barracks had been built everywhere, all around the racetrack and even in the infield.

Mr. Noma pointed beyond the track toward the horse stables. "I think your barrack is out there."

He was right. We came to a long stable that had once housed the horses of Tanforan, and we climbed up the wide ramp. Each stall had a number painted on it, and when we got to 40, Mr. Noma pushed open the door.

"Well, here it is," he said, "Apartment 40."

The stall was narrow and empty and dark. There were two small windows on each side of the door. Three folded army cots were on the dust-covered floor and one light bulb dangled from the ceiling. That was all. This was our apartment, and it still smelled of horses.

Mama looked at my sister and then at me. "It won't be so bad when we fix it up," she began. "I'll ask Mrs. Simpson to send me some material for curtains. I could make some cushions too, and . . .

well . . ." She stopped. She couldn't think of anything more to say.

Mr. Noma said he'd go get some mattresses for us. "I'd better hurry before they're all gone." He rushed off. I think he wanted to leave so that he wouldn't have to see Mama cry. But he needn't have run off, because Mama didn't cry. She just went out to borrow a broom and began sweeping out the dust and dirt. "Will you girls set up the cots?" she asked.

It was only after we'd put up the last cot that I noticed my bracelet was gone. "I've lost Laurie's bracelet!" I screamed. "My bracelet's gone!"

We looked all over the stall and even down the ramp. I wanted to run back down the track and go over every inch of ground we'd walked on, but it was getting dark and Mama wouldn't let me.

I thought of what I'd promised Laurie. I wasn't ever going to take the bracelet off, not even when I went to take a shower. And now I had lost it on my very first day in camp. I wanted to cry.

I kept looking for it all the time we were in Tanforan. I didn't stop looking until the day we were sent to another camp, called Topaz, in the middle of a desert in Utah. And then I gave up.

But Mama told me never mind. She said I didn't need a bracelet to remember Laurie, just as I didn't need anything to remember Papa or our home in Berkeley or all the people and things we loved and had left behind.

"Those are things we can carry in our hearts and take with us no matter where we are sent," she said.

And I guess she was right. I've never forgotten Laurie, even now.

from Rescue: The Story of How Gentiles Saved Jews in the Holocaust

by Milton Meltzer

In 1938 Oskar Schindler, a wealthy young German industrialist and card-carrying member of the Nazi party, was on the fast track. All he cared about was success, money, women, and having a luxurious lifestyle. However, when the Holocaust began, Schindler turned all of his energies to keeping as many Jews from the concentration camps as he could, using whatever means at his disposal.

Oskar Schindler: drinker, womanizer, gambler, profiteer, briber, wheeler-dealer, Nazi. It does not read like the description of a saint. Nor was he one. Yet he saved human souls, 1,200 of them. Where did he come from? How did he become a man of honor?

Oskar was born in 1908, in the small industrial city of Zwittau, then part of the Austrian empire. (Ten years later, after World War I, it became part of the new nation of Czechoslovakia.) His father owned a farm machinery plant and Oskar was trained to be an engineer. The Schindler family was Catholic, but young Oskar cared little about religion. Among his friends were a few Jewish classmates at the German grammar school. More interested in racing, Oskar built his own motorcycle and competed on mountain courses.

At the age of twenty, he married Emilie, a gentleman farmer's daughter. She was a quiet girl schooled in a convent. They seemed to have little in common. But who could resist tall, handsome Oskar? His magnetic charm was always successful with women. Now of draft age, Oskar was called into military service. He detested everything about it except the chance to drive a truck. After completing his service, he went home again and he worked for his father. But the factory went bankrupt during the depression of the 1930s. Oskar glided right into a job as a sales manager of an electrical company. He liked going out on the road, selling, meeting new people—especially women. What made his job easier was joining the local Nazi party. The Nazi badge helped get orders when he visited German companies.

In 1938 Hitler's troops marched into Czechoslovakia. Being a Nazi didn't look so good to Oskar now. He was shocked by the brutal way the Germans forcibly removed Jews and Czechs from those areas considered German and their grabbing of Czech and Jewish property. His wife Emilie thought Hitler would surely be punished for making himself God; his father believed Hitler, like Napoleon, would wind up a nobody. Oskar began to lose his zeal for the new order.

One evening, at a party, Oskar met a pleasant young German who talked business and politics with him as they drank alone in a side room. Growing confident with Oskar, the man identified himself as an officer in the Abwehr, the German Intelligence corps. You travel in Poland for your company, he said; why not supply the Abwehr with military and industrial information about that region? You'll be excused from military service, of course, if you become our agent. That made the proposal quite attractive to Oskar. He didn't worry about a military takeover of Poland. Not then.

A year later the invasion of Poland succeeded easily. And soon after, Oskar arrived in Cracow, a beautiful medieval city of Poland, ringed by metal, textile, and chemical plants. There he took charge of a factory that would make mess kits and field kitchenware for the German army.

Oskar settled comfortably into an elegant neighborhood of Cracow, his expensive clothes and sleek chauffeured car matching the high style of his apartment. While his wife Emilie stayed at home in Moravia, he kept house with a German mistress and conducted an affair with his Polish secretary at the factory office.

Only a short distance from Cracow was the forced labor camp at Plaszow, the barbed-wire home of 20,000 Jews. Oskar was friendly with its chief, Amon Goeth, as well as with the district heads of the various Nazi security forces. Oskar once had been a salesman. Now in Cracow he was a tycoon, operating in a boom time. The contracts he got to manufacture the products that the German forces needed brought in big profits. Oskar worked inside a corrupt and savage system and knew how to use its every rotten device for his own ends. He dealt cleverly on the black market, enjoying a talent for acquiring luxuries—silk, furniture, jewelry, clothing, liquor. Some for himself, some to seduce Nazis in high places. Their friendship kept him out of the army. Why waste such a generous man on the battlefield?

But as Oskar saw the sporadic Nazi raids and killing of Jews increase, his "friends" began to rouse a deep disgust in him. He knew how the SS would sweep into a Jewish street, break into apartments, loot them of all they contained, rip jewelry off fingers and throats, break an arm or a leg of anyone who hid something, shoot anyone they pleased. One day an SS squad invaded a fourteenth-century synagogue. They lined up the Jews they found at prayer, dragged in Jewish passersby, and made them all file past the Torah and spit on it. When one Jew refused to spit on the scroll, they shot him. Then they shot all the others and burned down Poland's oldest synagogue. As the silent aim of the Nazis—to exterminate all the Jews—became clear to Oskar, a cold rage seized him. Were these German massacres of Jews the actions of a *civilized* nation? What could end this madness?

When Oskar took over the Cracow factory it had only forty-five workers. As his army contracts swelled, their number grew to 250. His accountant was a Jew, Itzhak Stern. Stern asked him to hire this Jewish friend, then that one, then still another, and soon Oskar had 150 Jews in his employ. In the spring of 1941 the Nazis ordered all Jews out of Cracow, all but five or six thousand skilled ones needed for the war effort. These were shoved behind ghetto walls. Oskar's plant became a haven for Jews claiming such skills. Those who worked for Oskar had a blue sticker that enabled them to go in and out of the ghetto to work.

A little later Oskar made a deal with the German armaments people to add a munitions section to his plant to make antitank shells. This was better than making only pots and pans, for now who could question that he had a really essential industry?

Oskar added a night shift, and took on more Jews. "You'll be safe working here," he told them. "If you work here, you'll live through the war." How could they believe that promise? Who was this young blond giant—he was only thirty-four—who made such promises? But Oskar's calm certainty made them believe. And they wanted to, of course.

Oskar went on making his deals. And through his close connections with the local Nazi hierarchy, he often learned of their plans and passed the information on to the Jews who worked for him. He did business with the SS man who ran the ghetto, Julian Scherner. Scherner liked women, booze, luxuries, all the good things that came with his new power. And he seemed to prefer working the Jews to killing them. Oskar made good use of Scherner to get still more Jews onto his work rolls.

When rumors started to fly that the ghetto would gradually be "eliminated," Oskar convinced Scherner to let him set up cots in his plant so his night shift wouldn't be interrupted. That got some of his Jews out of the ghetto. But many others were still inside.

One day Oskar learned that a number of his workers, including his office manager, Abraham Bankier, had been taken out of the ghetto along with a great many other Jews and marched off to the railroad. Oskar drove at once to the depot, and found the Jews boarding a long string of cattle cars. Bound for where? For what? No one seemed to know. A labor camp, someone guessed. Oskar had recently seen an SS bulletin asking for bids to build crematoria in Belzec, a camp southeast of Lublin. Could this be the destination of these Jews? He ran down the track, calling out Bankier's name. He found him and the other twelve of his workers huddled together in the corner of one car. Then, by bluff and bribe, he got the SS to scratch the thirteen names off the shipping list on the grounds that a mistake had been made about these essential munitions workers.

As Oskar watched Jews taken out of the ghetto and marched to the cattle cars, he could not fail to guess what the end would be. The proof came when Bachner, a young Jewish pharmacist who had been shipped off, returned to the ghetto eight days later. He had seen the final horror. The Cracow Jews had been taken to Belzec, stripped naked, their heads shaved, and forced into "bathhouses," where they were gassed. All but him. Somehow he had gotten to a latrine and dropped into its pit, hiding there three days in human waste up to his neck. At last he was able to climb out in the dark and slip out of the camp. Because the Cracow ghetto was the only home he knew, he had walked the tracks right back into it. Now everyone in the ghetto knew the truth.

Twice in 1942 Oskar was arrested by the Gestapo on suspicion of wrongdoing. But each time he was sprung from prison by his influential friends, and he went on protecting the Jews in his factory. Their living and working conditions were humane. They were spared the atrocities of the Plaszow labor camp, and whenever the SS ordered a few of his Jews to Plaszow, he always found a way to rescue them. His generosity to SS officials on their birthdays became legendary.

Oskar's factory now employed 550 Jews, for whose labor he paid the SS a fixed rate of so much per day per person. In the autumn of 1942 a Zionist courier came to see Oskar. Someone (perhaps Itzhak Stern) had sent word abroad to Jewish organizations that Oskar was a righteous person, a man to be trusted. The world knew nothing but rumors of what Hitler was doing to the Jews of Europe. Oskar, sitting in the heart of the German territories, the confidant of the SS, could tell them. He did, giving the courier his eyewitness account, exaggerating nothing. Then he agreed to travel to Budapest to give Jewish leaders the first full-scale report they would have on the Polish horror.

The Cracow ghetto was nearing its end. The Germans had expanded Plaszow to take in thousands more Jews, and in March 1943 the ghetto was finally closed. The Jews still able to work were marched into Plaszow. The others—the old, sick, unemployable—were shot in their beds or shipped to Auschwitz. For more than seven centuries there had been a Jewish Cracow. Now Cracow was *judenrein*—free of Jews.

Oskar soon learned that Plaszow would be used not only as a forced labor camp but also as a place of execution. Everyone behind the wire was under sentence of death. Today? Tomorrow? It was just a question of when.

Oskar had been assured that his workers living in Plaszow would always arrive on time for their scheduled shifts in his factory. But now all sorts of things held them up. Complaints got him nowhere. So he came up with a bold idea. Why not build a subcamp where his workers could live in his own factory yard? He convinced the Plaszow commander that it made sense. Why not? Oskar could make his Jews work all the harder, and think of the money to be saved; he would feed his Jews at his own expense, and pay for the cost of building the new subcamp. A good fellow, this Schindler, the Nazis said, even if he was infected with that crazy disease of "Jew love"! Besides, Jews from other ghettos to be abolished were to be moved into Plaszow, and Oskar's subcamp would leave room in Plaszow for some of these newcomers.

So up went six new barracks to house 1,200 people. A cookhouse too, and a good shower block, and a laundry. Schindler's Jews knew what they had been given: no SS officer to brutalize them, no guards inside the camp, only at the entrance; a kitchen that supplied more and better soup and bread than in Plaszow. There were long work shifts, yes, but profits had to be made if the factory was to survive. No one died of overwork or hunger or beatings. (Compare it to the forced labor plant run for the giant German chemical firm I.G. Farben, where two out of three died at their labor.) A "paradise," the prisoners thought, a magical paradise that had sprung up here in the midst of hell.

It was not beyond Oskar's daring to contrive a way to photograph the inside workings of Plaszow. He got a written permit from his friend the SS commandant to take two "brother industrialists" on a tour of the "model industrial community." Both men, carrying proper passports, were secret agents of a Jewish rescue organization that wanted visual evidence for the world outside. With Itzhak Stern at his side, Oskar conducted the two men through the camp, as a minicamera captured scene after scene of the killing labor, of the scarred and starving prisoners, of the bloodied wheelbarrows used to transport the dead, and of the mass graves where they lay.

In April 1944, as Oskar reached his thirty-sixth birthday, the Russians rapidly moved west on the offensive. The SS was busy emptying the death camps. They dynamited the gas chambers and crematoria, to leave no recognizable trace. In

Plaszow they were burning bodies, thousands of them, immediately after killings. Those buried earlier in the woods were dug up and burned, to remove the evidence of mass murder.

Cracow was alive with rumors. Plaszow would be closed, Oskar learned. Then came an order from the Director of Armaments: Oskar's subcamp would be closed too, and the prisoners would go back into Plaszow, to await "relocation." He knew what that word meant: extermination. The news ripped through his barracks. It's the end, the Jews said. Oskar had given them some safety and sanity. Now they would all die.

Not if Oskar could prevent it. Let me move my factory west to Czechoslovakia, he said to the SS. And let me take my skilled workers with me, along with others in Plaszow whose special talents I could use.

It's all right with me, said SS officer Amon Goeth, smelling out big gifts from Oskar, so long as you get the cooperation you'll need from all the other authorities.

Oskar began preparing a list of people to be moved to wherever the new plant would be. Rumors of the plan reached his workshops. A Schindler list was in the making! Everyone prayed to be on it.

It took rapid maneuvers and handsome bribes to push his plan through. Finally the Berlin bigwigs agreed that Oskar's armaments plant would be moved to an annex of a spinning mill in Brinnlitz, a German village in Moravia, near Oskar's birthplace. Speed was vital; any delays would put his Jewish workers into Auschwitz.

The men on the Schindler list, numbering about 800 (the 300 women were to come on another train), boarded freight cars for Brinnlitz in mid-October

1944. After a hard journey, with long delays en route, they reached Brinnlitz and saw the new labor camp, with watchtowers, wire fence, guard barracks at the gate, and beyond it, the factory and the prisoners' dormitories. There in the courtyard, waiting to greet them, stood Oskar, a splendid sight in his Tyrolean hat, the hat he wore to celebrate his return home to his native mountains.

The new camp had been built at tremendous cost, Oskar's cost. Yet now he had no intention of producing anything useful to the Nazis. Four years earlier, arriving in Cracow, he had meant to get rich. He no longer had any desire to make profits out of slave labor. His personal life had changed too; Emilie, his wife, had come from Zwittau to live with him.

The prisoners quickly sensed that Oskar no longer cared about war production. They worked slowly, and no one speeded them up. The Brinnlitz SS garrison was made up of middle-aged men, reservists called up to replace the younger and more brutal SS men sent to the front lines. They too knew the war was winding down and Germany was losing. They were content to stay out of Oskar's way and not bother his workers.

Then Oskar was arrested again, a third time. The Gestapo handcuffed him and took him back to Cracow. For seven days they grilled him, seeking proof of corruption. But soon his friends in high places stepped in again to vouch for his honesty and loyalty, and on the eighth day they let him go. But while he was in prison, it turned out that Emilie, whom everyone had dismissed as a dull and compliant housewife, had taken over and carried on with Oskar's plans. Not because she was his wife. But because she too cared. She too was committed to human decency.

Oskar was not intimidated by his most recent arrest. His next exploit was to remove from Auschwitz the 300 women who had been on his list in Cracow. They had been slated to go with the other Jews to Brinnlitz. Instead, their train had carried them into Auschwitz. When the car doors opened, the terrified women asked themselves what this meant. Under the floodlights prisoners were sorted out. SS women pointed to them and told the uniformed doctors, These are *Schindlergruppe*. And they were marched off to barracks in the women's camp.

They learned they were marked as a reserve group of "industrial prisoners." Others with that same designation had not been spared, but had disappeared into the killing machine. Weeks passed. The Schindler women, sick, weakened, moved toward death. Some asked, "Where's Schindler now?" Would he keep his promises? But most of them did not despair. In Brinnlitz the men pressed Oskar, "Where are our women?" "I'm getting them out," he answered.

How he succeeded no one is sure. Who had ever heard of anyone being rescued from Auschwitz? The myth already wrapping Oskar's actions in mystery clouded his moves. What seems certain, however, is that Oskar had several telephone conversations with Rudolf Höss, the head of Auschwitz, and two of his chief officers. When the moment seemed ripe, Oskar sent a young woman with a load of liquor, ham, and diamonds to complete a deal with the functionaries. And sometime in November, the *Schindlerfrauen* were called out of their barracks, were showered in a washhouse, had their skulls shaved, and then were marched naked to a quartermaster's hut where they were handed the odds and ends of the clothing of the dead. Half dead themselves, dressed in rags, they were packed tight into the darkness of freight cars. The train rolled out of Auschwitz. In the cold dawn of the next day they were ordered out at a rural siding. Shivering, coughing, they stumbled ahead to a large gate guarded by SS men. Behind the gate rose tall brick chimneys. Panic seized them: Was this another death factory? But as they reached the gate, they could see Oskar standing in the midst of the SS men. He stepped forward to greet the women. "You have nothing more to worry about," he said. "You're with me now." One of them remembered years later that on seeing him she felt that "he was our father, he was our mother, he was our only faith. He never let us down."

Oskar wandered all over Moravia, buying food for his Jews, and arms and ammunition so they could defend themselves in case the SS tried to kill them during a retreat. His factory still produced nothing. Or almost nothing. They did ship one truckload of antitank shells so badly made that they were returned because they failed quality control tests. Good, said Oskar when an official complaint was made, now I know nobody has been killed by my product.

How did his factory pass inspection? For there were plenty of inspectors sent in routinely. Just as routinely, Oskar dined them and liquored them up so richly they scarcely knew what they were looking at in his workshops. And off they went, loaded with gifts of cigarettes and cognac. Some said he bought shells from other Czech factories and passed them off as his own if an inspector really tried to look at something. Whatever Oskar's confidence tricks were, they worked.

Then on May 7, 1945, the prisoners heard BBC radio broadcast the news of the German surrender. The war in Europe would end at midnight on May 8th. Oskar already knew the Russians were about to enter Brinnlitz. Somehow he had to avoid them and reach the Americans, where he might hope for better treatment. But first, with the SS guards present, he spoke to the prisoners. He invited the SS to leave, and asked the prisoners to let them go. The SS men dropped their weapons at the gate, and by midnight all had gone.

Next, Oskar and Emilie prepared to leave. They put on prisoner's stripes, and eight Jews volunteered to travel with them, to protect these two Germans from anyone who might try to harm them. They carried with them a letter attesting to the record of the Schindlers' good deeds all these years.

It was hard for the other prisoners to say good-bye. They handed Oskar a gift. It was a ring made of gold donated from the bridgework of a Jewish prisoner. On it they had inscribed this Talmudic verse: "Whoever saves a single soul, it is as if he had saved the whole world."

On the road they ran into an American infantry battalion, which included several Jewish soldiers and a field rabbi. When the Americans heard the Schindler story from the Jews, they embraced Oskar. He was safe.

Everything Oskar had owned was confiscated by the Russians. He was penniless. But his "family"—the *Schindlerjuden* (Schindler's Jews), as they proudly called themselves—would care for him the rest of his life. He and Emilie took up farming in Argentina for ten years, then went back to Germany. Oskar never prospered again. He became more dependent on the survivors, who gave him financial and emotional support.

In 1961 he visited Israel as a guest of the *Schindlerjuden,* and was welcomed ecstatically by the public and the press. "We do not forget the sorrows of Egypt, we do not forget Haman, we do not forget Hitler. Among the unjust, we do not forget the just. Remember Oskar Schindler."

In 1974 he died in Germany. At his request, he was buried in the Latin Cemetery in Jerusalem.

Acknowledgments

(continued from page ii)

Houghton Mifflin Company: "Bubili: A Gypsy's Fight for Survival," from *The Other Victims* by Ina R. Friedman. Copyright © 1990 by Ina R. Friedman. Reprinted by permission of Houghton Mifflin Company. All rights reserved.

The Bancroft Library for the Estate of Yoshiko Uchida: "The Bracelet," from *Japanese Journey: The Story of a People* by Yoshiko Uchida. Reprinted by permission of The Bancroft Library, University of California, Berkeley, for the Estate of Yoshiko Uchida.

HarperCollins Publishers: "Schindler's Jews," from *Rescue: The Story of How Gentiles Saved Jews in the Holocaust* by Milton Meltzer. Copyright © 1988 by Milton Meltzer. Reprinted by permission of HarperCollins Publishers.

Jessica B. Smith: "Elegy for Anne Frank," from *Literary Cavalcade*, 1990. Reprinted by permission of Jessica B. Smith.